To our friend and colleague from Down
Under, Elaine Brownlow—

Championing thoughtful schools for over
twenty years and still working to
Catch Them Thinking!

7 Key Student Proficiencies of the New National Standards

How to Teach
Thinking Skills
Within the
Common Core

James A. Bellanca • Robin J. Fogarty • Brian M. Pete

Solution Tree | Press

a division of

Solution Tree

555 North Morton Street
Bloomington, IN 47404
800.733.6786 (toll free) / 812.336.7700
FAX: 812.336.7790

email: info@solution-tree.com
solution-tree.com

Visit **go.solution-tree.com/commoncore** to download the reproducibles and access live links to the websites in this book.

Printed in the United States of America

16 15 14 13 12   2 3 4 5

Library of Congress Cataloging-in-Publication Data

Bellanca, James A., 1937- author.
   How to teach thinking skills within the common core : 7 key student proficiencies of the new national standards / James A. Bellanca, Robin J. Fogarty, Brian M. Pete.
      pages cm
   Includes bibliographical references and index.
   ISBN 978-1-936764-07-5 (perfect bound) -- ISBN 978-1-936764-08-2 (library bound)
1. Thought and thinking--Study and teaching. I. Fogarty, Robin, author. II. Pete, Brian M., author. III. Title.
   LB1590.3.B45 2012
   370.15'2--dc23
                          2012013920

Solution Tree

Jeffrey C. Jones, CEO
Edmund M. Ackerman, President

Solution Tree Press

President: Douglas M. Rife
Publisher: Robert D. Clouse
Vice President of Production: Gretchen Knapp
Managing Production Editor: Caroline Wise
Senior Production Editor: Lesley Bolton
Proofreader: Rachel Rosolina
Text Designer: Rian Anderson
Cover Designer: Amy Shock

Acknowledgments

Since publishing our first multiple-edition book together in 1987, much has transpired. With that first book, *Patterns for Thinking*, we wanted to provide information that enabled classroom teachers to take the ideas presented and move them right to their classrooms. We also wanted a book that could help with the emerging role of "staff developers" as teachers of teachers. Since then, we have collaborated on many books, always keeping in mind the value of transforming theory into practice so that classrooms might become more thoughtful places.

Although *Patterns* focused on thinking, it was built on the just-emerging cooperative learning research of Roger and David Johnson. Their understanding of cooperative learning as a bed for critical thinking, conflict resolution, and problem solving made a substantive foundation for creating the classroom environment supportive of the ideas we wanted to communicate.

Early on, Art Costa, David Perkins, and John Barell entered the conversation and inspired Robin to research transfer theory, especially concerning thinking skills and problem solving. Her doctoral study took on a practical tone when we used it over and over to inform our professional development work. When Robin interpreted the Oliver Wendell Holmes quote that described three-story intellects at their peak, looking through a skylight to wonder at the stars in the heavens, her descriptions of transfer in practice set us on a path that continues today.

Thus, for this book, we must acknowledge first the support staff at Skylight Professional Development, especially Mary Jane Bloethner, Donna Ramirez, Dave Stockman, Bruce Leckie, Julie Noblit, Amy Wolgemuth, Monica Phillips, and Jean Ward. To these, we add the full-time professional team of colleagues who comprised the famous think tank that Skylight nurtured and embraced: Kay Burke, Carolyn Chapman, Bruce Williams, Beth Swartz, Meir Ben Hur—and the consultants who grew with us as authors and professional developers, Sue Marcus Augustine, Penny Finely, Valerie Gregory, Carol Scearce, Gayle Gregory, Terry Perry, Donna Wilson, and Eleanor Renee Rodriquez.

Like Dorothy finding many friends along the yellow brick road, we expanded our list of friends, mentors, and collaborators. In addition to the mentioned colleagues who have remained with us for so long, others have joined the list and provided voices to deepen our understanding of best practice and theory. Those voices most deserving of our thanks include Ron Brandt, Howard Gardner, Reuven Feuerstein, Bob Sternberg, Bob Garmston, Merrill Harmin, Howard Kirschenbaum, Jay McTighe, Laura Lipton, Charlotte Danielson, Elaine Brownlow, and Faye Hauwai.

In this publication, you may hear these many voices speaking here and there. Equally important, you will see the model we have refined over and over to transfer what we have learned over the years into more practical professional learning experiences that move easily into classroom practice. In essence, we see this book as a funnel for not only the best practices for improving achievement and advancing students' 21st century skills, especially the core skill of critical thinking, but also the best practices of professional learning that are most likely to empower teachers and administrators to make good sense of the Common Core State Standards.

Finally, we must acknowledge our publication team at Solution Tree. We start with Jeff Jones, CEO extraordinaire, and his best practice of treating authors with a unique respect and providing the support and expertise of an unsurpassed publication staff. To Solution Tree Press President Douglas Rife and renowned publisher Robb Clouse, who together have the eyes and ears for just the right titles; Gretchen Knapp and Lesley Bolton, who drive the book to its conclusion; and Claudia Wheatley, who supports the work with passion and panache, we extend our heartfelt gratitude. We humbly acknowledge the role each plays in transferring the ethereal words that percolate in our heads to everlasting words on paper for others.

Jim, Robin, and Brian

Chicago, Illinois

2012

Solution Tree Press would like to thank the following reviewers:

Kristina Blair
Third- and Fourth-Grade Teacher
Franklin Elementary
Massillon, Ohio

Patricia A. Paxton
Fifth-Grade Teacher
Krause Later Elementary
Armada, Michigan

Rebecca Stinson
Principal
Claremont Math, Science, and Technology Academy
Chicago, Illinois

Lindi Wilson
Fifth-Grade Teacher
Princeton Elementary
Birmingham, Alabama

Visit **go.solution-tree.com/commoncore**
*to download the reproducibles and access live
links to the websites in this book.*

Table of Contents

> *Reproducible pages are in italics.*

4 Comprehensive Thinking   89

7   Cognitive Transfer   161

About the Authors

 **James A. Bellanca** is founder and CEO of International Renewal Institute and founder of the educational publishing company Skylight. His extensive experience as a classroom teacher, alternative school director, professional developer, and intermediate service center consultant has given him a wide scope of knowledge. Known for his cutting-edge program design and implementation of research-rich, standards-aligned professional learning programs for educators, Jim has worked with educational leaders in districts across the United States to design programs that promote critical thinking and collaboration to increase academic performance among all children, including high-risk student populations.

In addition to his other accomplishments, Jim has designed alternative school programs; an intermediate service center that pioneered practical professional development programs; a statewide, strategy-based set of courses for teachers; Illinois's largest and most dynamic field-based master's degree program (in partnership with three universities); and a nonprofit service agency dedicated to the development of a 21st century enriched learning school model based on the full integration of the Feuerstein method across all areas of curriculum and instruction. Jim is the author of *Enriched Learning Projects: A Practical Pathway to 21st Century Skills* and is the editor, with Ron Brandt, of *21st Century Skills*. He serves as the executive director of the Illinois Consortium for 21st Century Skills and writes the blog *Connecting the 21st Century Dots: From Policy to Practice* for the Partnership for 21st Century Skills.

Robin J. Fogarty, PhD, is president of Robin Fogarty & Associates, a Chicago-based, minority-owned educational publishing and consulting company. Her doctorate is in curriculum and human resource development from Loyola University of Chicago. A leading proponent of the thoughtful classroom, Robin has trained educators throughout the world in curriculum, instruction, and assessment strategies. She has taught at all levels, from kindergarten to college; served as an administrator; and consulted with state departments and ministries of education in the United States, Puerto Rico, Russia, Canada, Australia, New Zealand, Germany, Great Britain, Singapore, Korea, and the Netherlands. Robin has published articles in *Educational Leadership*, *Phi Delta Kappan*, and the *Journal of Staff Development*. She is the author of numerous publications, including *Brain-Compatible Classrooms*, *Ten Things New Teachers Need*, *Literacy Matters*, *How to Integrate the Curricula*, *Close the Achievement Gap*, *Informative Assessment: When It's Not About a Grade*, *Twelve Brain Principles That Make the Difference*, and *Nine Best Practices That Make the Difference*. Her recent work includes the two-book leadership series, *From Staff Room to Classroom*, and *Supporting Differentiated Instruction: A Professional Learning Communities Approach*.

Brian M. Pete is cofounder of Robin Fogarty & Associates, an educational consulting and publishing company. He comes from a family of educators—college professors, school superintendents, teachers, and teachers of teachers. He has a rich background in professional development. Brian has worked with and taped classroom teachers and professional experts in schools throughout the United States, Europe, Asia, Australia, and New Zealand. He has an eye for the "teachable moment" and the words to describe what he sees as skillful teaching. Brian's educational videos include *Best Practices: Classroom Management* and *Best Practices: Active Learning Classrooms*. He is coauthor of eleven books, which include *Data! Dialogue! Decisions!*, *Twelve Brain Principles That Make the Difference*, *Nine Best Practices That Make the Difference*, *The Adult Learner*, *A Look at Transfer*, and *From Staff Room to Classroom I* and *II*. His most recent publication is *Supporting Differentiated Instruction: A Professional Learning Communities Approach*.

To book James A. Bellanca, Robin J. Fogarty, or Brian M. Pete for professional development, contact pd@solution-tree.com.

Introduction

In the days of one-room schoolhouses, there were no standards; teachers invented the curriculum. By the 20th century, teachers were asked to follow curriculum guides. As they worked tirelessly to deliver their instruction, wanting only to ensure every student was succeeding, teachers often dropped the lightly used guides into the bottom desk drawer.

More recently, each state created its own standards so that its teachers could have consistent goals. However, across the states, there was little agreement and even less consistency. Each state did its own thing; the college and career readiness of high school graduates in one state varied greatly from that of other states. A look back at a prior round of standards uncovers a second deficiency. Because there were no adequate tools to test the thinking elements that were included in these earlier standards, states bought or prepared their own tests based on what was "testable" in the standards. Instead of testing the highest expectations of rigorous student cognition, test makers gravitated to the lowest common denominator. Their tests looked to the facts of information that could be measured. Because assessment drives instruction and No Child Left Behind (NCLB) procedures rewarded high test scores, it wasn't long before school districts, aided by publishers and their test companies, drove instruction into the land of test prep: fill-in-the-blanks were substituted for guided practice; scripts were created with methods that directed whole-class memory practices; and time was subtracted from the curriculum for day upon day of pretest practice. Very little time was left for critical thinking and problem solving in the daily classroom regimen.

In the first decade of the 21st century, multiple studies from such organizations as the American Management Association, National School Boards Association, National Education Association, McGraw Hill Research Group, the National Governors Association, the American College Testing Service, the Partnership for 21st Century Skills, and the Council of Chief State School Officers began to call for more rigorous, relevant, and results-directed curricula and instruction reforms that would return the four Cs—critical thinking, creative problem solving, collaboration, and communication—to daily instruction. Prominent educational authors such as

Linda Darling-Hammond, Tony Wagner, Charles Fadel, and Howard Gardner began to shout a common message. Globalization, they repeated, is demanding a drastically upgraded education. Burgeoning global economics have raised the level of schooling available to students in poor, underdeveloped countries to heights that are now surpassing the 20th century excellence of American schools. The studies argued that more of the same NCLB basics would not be sufficient to change the course. Any answer must enable our nation to meet global economic challenges with an educational response that will stimulate American students to continue thriving at the top (Partnership for 21st Century Skills, 2011).

In this century's second decade, the creation of a consistent, more rigorous set of national standards was a first response to the many cries for a substantive and balanced 21st century reform. The Common Core State Standards (CCSS; National Governors Association Center for Best Practices [NGA] & Council of Chief State School Officers [CCSSO], 2010a) are designed to make all students college and career ready in mathematics, reading, writing, speaking, and listening. This new iteration calls for teachers to prepare students with rich content knowledge and relevant thinking skills essential for success after high school in the 21st century. It eschews those low-expectation standards that claim that memorization of facts provides a sufficient education for succeeding in this complex new world.

The beat, however, goes on. The Programme for International Student Assessment (PISA) test that waved high the flag signaling the start of this closely watched global education comparison raised the ante with the publication of its frameworks for the 2012 tests. In addition to exams in literacy and mathematical problem solving, 2012 will initiate online exams of cross-curricular problem solving and financial literacy. By 2013, the thirty or more nations participating will be ranked, as in the past, against each other. As seen in its announcement of the tests, the cross-curricular problem-solving test will highlight ill-defined real-world problems at four levels of difficulty (Programme for International Student Assessment [PISA], 2012).

This is not the only red flag that the international competitions are likely to intensify in years to come. Other nations are working assiduously to improve their standing as global education leaders. For instance, Australia, one of the three highest performing nations on past PISA exams began its improvement task soon after the first PISA results appeared. Its major population states—South Australia, New South Wales, and Queensland—have prepared statewide programs with the aim of improving best classroom practice and results. South Australia's Department of Education and Children's services spent the last six years producing two leadership documents to guide schools with a comprehensive and detailed *Teaching and Effective Learning Framework*. The documents describe and provide tools for principals and teachers to collaborate in the development of classrooms pushed by high-quality best practices that promote the types of teaching and learning reflected in PISA's problem-solving emphasis (Atkins & Fisher, 2010, 2011).

If the goal of the CCSS is to help today's schools prepare all students to be college and career ready with rich and rigorous 21st century skills, the challenge is clearly based in answering the question, How can schools best take advantage of the standards in improving classroom instruction and curriculum aligned to 21st century demands? The answer, as noted, cannot be more of the same with content regurgitation serving as best practice. If students are to become productive problem solvers, sound decision makers, and creative innovators as called for by the many reports and educational experts, educators must include the explicit development of those complex thinking skills as the action antecedents to the stated content. Otherwise, the educational community will repeat the same mistakes made with its first move to a standards-based curriculum—namely, the creation of lofty and noble content standards assessed at the lowest levels of learning with classroom instruction reduced to test prep with skill-and-drill practice exercises that undermine the real goals of deep thinking about rich and rigorous content. Such a response certainly will not meet the high expectations crucial for today's students who must learn and work in the global world of tomorrow.

To guide their own use of the new standards, educators can start by asking profound questions, including:

- How do teachers embed these thinking skills into curricular content so that student achievement rises and all students have an equitable opportunity to develop the quality of their thinking and problem solving, not just for tests, but for a lifetime of learning?

- How do the new standards help teachers empower all learners with the discriminating and enduring skills of proficient thinkers, such as analyze critically, interpret meaning, determine evidence, discern themes, clarify relationships, and identify point of view, nuance, and bias?

- How do teachers make sure they are not falling to the low expectation of merely asking students to memorize facts and regurgitate figures?

In response to these questions, *How to Teach Thinking Skills Within the Common Core* identifies twenty-one complex cognitive skills that are most prominent within the new standards. It then generalizes these rigorous skills so they are approachable and applicable to every student, no matter what grade level or subject—and without loading extra busywork on teachers who already have more than enough planning to do. In this light, the book builds on teachers' prior knowledge so each teacher can focus on the specific standards that impact his or her classroom.

The book's practical approach refuses to turn the standards into a giant academic hurdle. Instead, it follows the age-old wisdom of KISS (keep it simple, stupid). In short, this book is designed to prepare teachers and their educational leaders to make simple adjustments to classroom instruction. It relies on a practical approach that will enhance both the critical thinking skills and the rigorous content these new standards bring to the classroom. Ultimately, it looks to assist today's students with the development of relevant life skills and rigorous knowledge that will best serve them through all of their school years. This is not teaching to the test. It is teaching for a lifetime.

A Practical and Explicit Exposition

This practical handbook is divided into seven student proficiencies: (1) critical thinking, (2) creative thinking, (3) complex thinking, (4) comprehensive thinking, (5) collaborative thinking, (6) communicative thinking, and (7) cognitive transfer. Tabs along the side of the book provide for quick access to each proficiency. Each proficiency identifies three essential thinking skills for explicit teaching, providing a manageable synthesis of the new standards. *Explicit* means that the skill is clearly and compactly defined so that a student has an unequivocal understanding of the term with nothing left to suggestion. In the explicit approach, teachers illuminate the targeted skill and teach a formal lesson about it. All attributes are identified, so there is no room for confusion or doubt about how to use the skill appropriately.

The twenty-one selected skills do not cover all the thinking skills in the standards. The majority of the skills selected were those most frequently captured in a keyword search of the standards. Others were selected because teachers indicated to the authors they were the most important thinking skills in their classrooms. Many of the thinking skills appear in the standards as explicit, first-word instructions—*analyze, solve, prove, interpret*. Others occur implicitly within the CCSS language. Throughout the book are feature boxes providing "Examples From the CCSS" that refer to the highlighted thinking skill. These example standards are taken directly from the CCSS and can be found at www.corestandards.org.

It is not this book's expectation that every teacher studies or implements every one of the twenty-one skills. Teachers' selections are best driven by their own grade-level and subject-area standards and the needs of their students. For implementation, less will be more, with each teacher focusing on the two or three key skills that he or she can develop with the deepest student competence and confidence over a school year.

In this book, each chapter targets one thinking skill. The skill is dissected for explicit teaching across elementary, middle, and secondary levels. The lessons target "process as content." In this way, instead of merely plucking an exemplar from the standards for test prep, teachers work through a process to unpack the complex thinking skills inherent in the core standards. In the end, by strengthening the students' complex thinking and problem solving skills, teachers enable students to deepen their comprehension of the text.

The Three-Phase Teaching Model

Each chapter follows a three-phase model for unpacking a skill. These three phases provide the road map for each explicit lesson. The model is an application of Lev Vygotsky's zone of proximal development theory, which calls for the gradual release of responsibility to the learners, empowering the learners to *own* their learning. It is a scaffolding approach that prepares the student for an independent path to mastery performance and strong transfer of learning. As explained by Douglas Fisher and Nancy Frey (2008), the gradual release of responsibility follows this path: I do, we do, you do together, you do alone. The teacher teaches the skill explicitly, demonstrating and vocalizing the learning; the teacher and student try it together, with the teacher monitoring and providing guidance; and finally, the student performs the skill on his or her own with confidence.

TALK THROUGH

Phase I—Talk-Through: Explicit Teaching Lesson

In phase I, the Talk-Through, the teacher explicitly presents the thinking skill in a formal lesson. This lesson focuses on a key idea, well-developed scaffolding, strategic integration, and adequate time for reflection and review. The goal is knowledge of the targeted skill—for instance, "What does it mean to analyze?"

The Talk-Through has five components:

1. Motivational mindset
2. Order of operations
3. Instructional strategy
4. Assessment
5. Metacognitive reflection

In this first phase, teachers engage students with a *motivational mindset*. This is a hook or advance organizer (Ausubel, 1960; Marzano, 1991), an activity that arouses interest and curiosity about the learning, stirs prior knowledge, and preferably provides an engaging hands-on experience that illuminates the skill in action. Next, the teacher delineates the thinking skill with an acronym called *order of operations*. This represents the cognitive procedures used for executing the thinking skill. The acronym serves to help both teachers and students easily remember the steps involved. After this introduction to the process, teachers present the user-friendly, high-energy *instructional strategy* that requires students to address the thinking skill, noting explicitly its parts and procedures and determining how the skill can be used across content areas and grade levels. Next, teachers ensure student understanding of the skill and its potential applications with the model's *assessment* suggestion. Finally, to bring closure to the explicit lesson, teachers offer a *metacognitive reflection* that acts as a deliberate look back on the learning of the skill and how it may affect students' lives.

WALK

THROUGH

Phase II—Walk-Through: Classroom Content Lesson

In phase II, the Walk-Through, teachers guide the practice of the thinking skill within content-based lessons, providing directed, collaborative support to ensure the students' appropriate application of the skill. To assist teachers with content and grade-appropriate lesson selections for this guided practice, each chapter provides strategies adaptable for all levels.

This phase includes the following:

1. Content lesson example for elementary level

2. Content lesson example for middle level

3. Content lesson example for secondary level

DRIVE

THROUGH

Phase III—Drive-Through: CCSS Performance Task Lesson

In phase III, the Drive-Through, the teacher helps individual students transfer their understanding of the thinking skill into authentic applications using performance tasks identified in the CCSS. In the English Language Arts (ELA) standards, the performance tasks are found in their Appendix B (NGA & CCSSO, 2010b). In the Math standards, the performance tasks are embedded in the standards themselves.

This phase includes the following:

1. CCSS performance task for elementary level

2. CCSS performance task for middle level

3. CCSS performance task for secondary level

With performance tasks, the opportunity for students to work on the tasks first in groups and then individually makes the gradual release of responsibility practical and possible. These joint tasks allow students to collaborate in making direct connections between the selected thinking skill, the new standards, and the rich application to rigorous texts before the final accountability step in which each student must show "I got it."

To guide the gradual release of responsibility, teachers create effective formative assessments that include the thinking skill. Prior to the final Drive-Through phase, the teacher creates a balanced rubric for formative assessments. This rubric will provide guiding criteria for both elements of the standard: the thinking process and the content. With minimal teacher guidance in this third phase, students should be able to identify the targeted thinking skill, construct the response as directed in the performance task, and guided by the rubric, self-assess and reflect on their work. When needed, teachers will provide additional performance tasks, coach, or make other interventions based on the progress students are making. As the quarter or semester continues, the teacher may add increasingly difficult tasks to the mix so that students are able to develop their standards-based thinking skills with more and more challenging content. In this way, the standards move from being a checklist to being a developmental guide that reveals the advances students make over the course of a quarter, a semester, or a year as they move to the final summative assessment of the grade-level standard.

The Teacher's Role in the Three Phases

When teachers intentionally release responsibility for learning tasks to the students, their instructional role changes. In phase I, the teacher models, explains, explicates, and enunciates instruction about the targeted skill. The teacher asks many productive questions, displays visuals, and listens to and clarifies student responses as she builds students' clear understanding of the skill's meaning. She defines, gives examples, checks for understanding, and assesses the students' knowledge of the skill. During this "teacher teaches student" phase, she may occasionally structure a cooperative learning task such as a think-pair-share but always with the purpose of helping all students gain a more exact grasp of the targeted skill's key attributes and best uses.

In this phase, two basic "I do and we do" models of instruction are helpful. Some teachers may be more comfortable relying on a traditional direct-instruction model. With the thinking skill as the content, these teachers will direct the class through phase I—hook, exposition and modeling of the operation, checking for understanding—until they can assess their students' grasp of the skill's definition and readiness for guided practice.

A second group of teachers will prefer to use inquiry-based instruction with more emphasis on the "we do" as the means of defining the key term. Their hook will be an essential question posed to the class (for example, What does it mean to analyze?). Often with students in their collaborative groups, these teachers will engage students in an exploratory activity that introduces the students to the thinking skill by "doing" it (for example, a mini-analysis of a familiar object) before they ask students, usually in teams, to identify key attributes of the cognitive experience (for example, "When you analyzed this story, what did you do? What steps did you take? What was help-ful?"). The teacher will then continue the more interactive "I do, we do" instruction with other collaborative strategies to illuminate the attributes identified and to help students form a final all-class answer to the essential question. With the answers syn-thesized by the teacher, the students are ready to take greater responsibility for their learning and practice embedding the skill in their course content.

In phase II, teachers take one step back from their direction of the class. The mix of "I do, we do" gives way to "we do, but alone." In this phase, the teachers increase the students' control of the learning activity. This is best done in collaborative groups that have been prepped to learn cooperatively (Johnson & Johnson, 1981).

It is important in this phase that the teacher's facilitation skills come to the fore and replace the telling and questioning models that dominated in the first phase. Her attention moves from individuals in the whole class to individuals in the small groups. She works at the side of the groups, moving from one to another—observing, checking for understanding, taking notes, coaching, cueing and questioning, mediat-ing students' thinking, and providing students with multiple opportunities to reflect on how successfully they are developing their thinking and are applying the new skills to the called-for curriculum content without providing answers or quick solutions. Facilitation serves as the heart of the purposeful guidance the teacher provides in this phase while observing progress or lack of progress, responding to a question on a student's face, providing feedback based on observation data, and moving students to higher levels of challenge with pertinent questions about their use of the skill in the assignment.

The line between what teachers do to facilitate practice in phase II and what they do to facilitate transfer in phase III is a matter of how the work is completed. In phase II, teachers have set up the situation for the student teams to practice embed-ding the targeted skill in a specified lesson with team members helping each other. Novice teams may work in pairs. More experienced teams may collaborate in groups of three or five. The teacher is not the sole helper because phase II teams help each other with the trial runs of the task. When teams get stuck, the teacher intervenes, first encouraging the students to figure out the problem. Only when they cannot does she step in to mediate their thinking.

After the teacher determines that her teams have sufficient practice to warrant independent application, she moves to phase III performance tasks. In these tasks, individuals take on the responsibility of completing the assignments. In a sense, these are guided pretest work. They show each student's ability to fulfill the standard at the level of expectation the teacher asks for. Using a rubric, the teacher can ask students to complete one or more standards-aligned performance tasks showing how well they can complete or address the thinking challenge with the assigned material. Ultimately, the teacher decides how many transfer tasks the student needs in order to reach the desired level of competence before a final assessment.

Among the three phases, there is no magic moment that indicates when the teacher's role changes. As teachers become more experienced with the nuances of the roles in each phase, they will develop a sense of what works best when.

A Road Map

Road maps (GPS maps in this age of technology) help travelers make long trips through unfamiliar territory to a wished-for destination. This book's road map (fig. I.1) displays the road trip that teachers will take from the beginning of a standards-aligned lesson or project to its end. The road map traces the learning progression for an entire explicit lesson about a targeted thinking skill from start to finish through the three phases. The display is designed so teachers can reproduce the list and write commentary to guide a skill's instruction through the three phases.

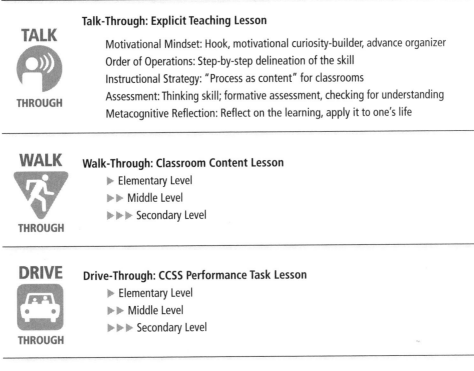

TALK THROUGH

Talk-Through: Explicit Teaching Lesson

Motivational Mindset: Hook, motivational curiosity-builder, advance organizer
Order of Operations: Step-by-step delineation of the skill
Instructional Strategy: "Process as content" for classrooms
Assessment: Thinking skill; formative assessment, checking for understanding
Metacognitive Reflection: Reflect on the learning, apply it to one's life

WALK THROUGH

Walk-Through: Classroom Content Lesson

▶ Elementary Level
▶▶ Middle Level
▶▶▶ Secondary Level

DRIVE THROUGH

Drive-Through: CCSS Performance Task Lesson

▶ Elementary Level
▶▶ Middle Level
▶▶▶ Secondary Level

Reflection Questions

Figure I.1: The Explicit Instruction Road Map.

In addition to the three-phase model, each chapter contains road signs that help mark the way. Each chapter begins with an introduction to the thinking skill, including a vignette that places the skill in a real-world setting, a definition of the skill, and examples of what the skill looks and sounds like in the classroom. At the end of each chapter, reflection questions help readers further personalize the chapter's information and learn from their own "doing."

A Note to the Reader

This book highlights the most crucial thinking skills students are now expected to acquire and use with accuracy and finesse, not just to pass the test, but to prepare for life, learning, and work after high school. It is complex, demanding work that increases the challenges of teaching.

Therefore, it may seem daunting to follow the three-phase model with twenty-one skills in seven student proficiencies. But it doesn't have to be. Start with attention to one skill. Since it is as unlikely that you will have to teach every skill as it is that you will have to teach every standard, focus on a few chapters that best align with your students' needs and your curriculum. Less is more.

To make your first skill choice, start with your grade's ELA or Mathematics standards. If you teach in another, non-mathematical subject area, simply go to the ELA informational text standards. Select a standard that makes you think: "Oh, yes, this is important for my students" or "Yep, this one gives my students lots of trouble." Identify the key word in that standard, then review this book's corresponding chapter with that standard in hand. Plan what you are going to do using the road map template, implement it, and assess the results. Once you have conquered this first skill, move on to the next and expand your repertoire.

How to Teach Thinking Skills Within the Common Core should become a well-thumbed resource for you and your colleagues as you balance teaching domain-specific content with the targeted, explicitly stated cognitive operations in the standards. The book is intended to be a user-friendly, practical guide that you can reference easily, whether scanning for the specific skill that needs attention or systematically addressing the skills through a synchronized effort by a professional learning community. It is designed to clarify the mass of information, both obvious and obscure, in the CCSS and to delineate an adaptable, practical approach to teaching the complex kinds of thinking represented in and supported by the new learning standards. Above all, it is meant to keep simple the adoption of the Common Core State Standards as a useful guide for daily instruction.

Following are a few things to keep in mind while reading:

- The standards in English are said to reflect some bias in favor of the traditional academic emphasis on expository writing and textual analysis. There is sure to be future debate around this vision of what is the best preparation for 21st century writing.

- English/language arts and mathematics are not the only subjects in the curriculum. Those who advocate for a curriculum that more closely aligns with the 21st century decry the reduction of science, social studies, and technology as subsets of the ELA standards. Others ask, Where are the visual arts, performing arts, and music arts?

- The biggest questions about the standards, any standards, are regarding their appropriate role in education. Are standards merely an extension of the factory model of learning that was favored in the 20th century? Are the standards just a tool to fix up and improve an overly scientific approach to teaching and learning that may be based on faulty theory and bad practice? What other alternative does our society have for ensuring that all students are prepared with the knowledge and skills that will give them the best chance to live, learn, and succeed in the coming decades?

The list of twenty-one skills is not the be-all and end-all of student proficiencies. Changes to the standards will undoubtedly come in the future as they did in the past. Hopefully, new iterations will continue to improve their worth to classroom teachers and improve the quality of the standards themselves.

Within the seven key student proficiencies, most of the skills were chosen due to their frequent occurrence in the CCSS (see table I.1, page 12). However, the following skills do not explicitly appear on the list: generate, associate, hypothesize, reason, connect, synthesize, and generalize. We have specifically included these because they are implied in the standards and performance tasks. Please note the following synonyms for these seven skills that do appear in the list: produce and create (generate); relationships and sequence (associate); predict and ask/answer (hypothesize); justify and demonstrate (reason); relationships and relate (connect); create and produce (synthesize); and comprehend and describe (generalize). One last note—a number of the previously listed skills are embedded in the creative production and presentation of performances required in CCSS exemplars and performance tasks. Thus, it seemed prudent to address the aspect that creativity plays in student achievement.

Table I.1: High-Frequency Words Within the Common Core State Standards

K–5				6–12			
ELA		**Math**		**ELA**		**Math**	
Understanding	33	Represent	47	Analyze	73	Solve	66
Read	28	Understand	40	Determine	50	Understand	54
Write	22	Solve	36	Develop	41	Interpret	47
Demonstrate	19	Recognize	27	Research	33	Relationships	45
Clarify	18	Interpret	22	Clarify	32	Find	43
Develop	18	Find	21	Write	31	Graph	39
Produce	17	Explain	20	Relationships	30	Represent	38
Relationships	16	Compare	19	Demonstrate	28	Apply	34
Describe	14	Describe	18	Understanding	27	Describe	24
Compare/contrast	13	Write	14	Create	26	Explain	23
Explain	13	Identify	12	Read	26	Prove	21
Answer	13	Understanding	11	Evaluate	22	Write	19
Introduce	10	Divide	9	Reflection	20	Compare/contrast	17
Sequence	10	Determine	9	Read/comprehend	20	Recognize	17
Produce	9	Graph	9	Introduce	17	Evaluate	13
Determine	8	Apply	9	Produce	17	Determine	13
Accurately	8	Sequence	7	Organize	17	Identify	11
Read/comprehend	8	Read	5	Point of view	15	Compute	10
Point of view	8	Answer	5	Apply	14	Develop	9
Apply	7	Create	5	Compare/contrast	12	Produce	8
Research/projects	6	Justify	4	Explain	11	Inferences	8
Create	6	Analyze	4	Inferences for text	10	Analyze	7
Decode	6	Develop	3	Sequence	9	Sequence	7
Reflection	5	Compute	2	Identify	8	Divide	7
Retell	4	Relationships	2	Solve	8	Calculate	7
Recall	4	Define	2	Projects	8	Decide	7
Sequences	4	Evaluate	1	Answer	8	Define	6
Inferences	4	Produce	1	Sequences	7	Answer	5
Identify	4	Calculate	1	Accurately	7	Create	4
Collaborate	3	Sequences	1	Interpret	6	Verify	3
Organize	3	Organize	1	Collaborate	3	Sequences	3
Ask/answer	3			Reflect	3	Justify	2
Short research	3					Read	2
Interpret	3					Understanding	1
Know and use	3					Reflection	1
Analyze	2						
Solve	1						

Critical Thinking

Critical thinking was central to great teaching in the days of the Greek philosophers Plato and Aristotle. Aristotle set the course of Western education by defining the educated mind and setting a standard of action by telling us that no idea should go unchallenged. The English essayist Francis Bacon introduced the "how to" for challenging ideas when he wrote, "Read not to contradict and confute; nor to believe and take for granted; nor to find talk and discourse; but to weigh and consider" (Bacon, 1625). More recently, Jean Piaget brought his prodigious mind to the subject when he said, "The principal goal of education in the schools should be creating men and women who are capable of doing new things, not simply repeating what other generations have done; men and women who are creative, inventive and discoverers, who can be critical and verify, and not accept, everything they are offered" (as quoted in Jervis & Tobier, 1988, p. 30).

None of these students of learning seem to advocate for more memory, more drills, or more reduction of the curriculum to facts and procedures to be tested so teachers can find the one correct answer regurgitated on a standardized test. Instead, they hold high expectations for the development of students' minds by challenging ideas; by weighing and considering; by creating, inventing, and discovering; and by being critical. For this, they know that teachers need the resources to engage their students in thinking about important, relevant issues, never to "accept everything they are offered."

For those who hope to advance their education beyond high school and into college or to compete for a significant job in the new global economy, the ability to think critically is a well-recognized imperative and an essential part of this century's first set of Common Core State Standards.

Critical thinking is the brick and mortar of problem solving and decision making. In this student proficiency, three skills spring forward. First, the quintessential critical thinking skill of _analyzing_ initiates the study of left-brain or inside-the-box thinking skills that saturate the CCSS. The standards also call for students to spend a large amount of time _evaluating_ and _problem solving_, the other two skills explored in this proficiency.

The interdependent nature of these key critical thinking skills is made apparent in the sample performance tasks for the English Language Arts standards. In the sample performance tasks related to stories, dramas, and poetry, students will complete the assessment with the most significant results because they are more skilled in knowing how to analyze, evaluate, and problem solve.

Mathematics and content areas also require students to think critically. They explicitly ask students to analyze for nuance; to evaluate point of view, evidence, and perspective or bias; and to solve problems some of which are tight and well defined and others of which are loose or ill defined.

When students develop their proficiency with these intertwined three skills through explicit instruction that deepens their understanding of the content in the standards, teachers can return to the high expectations of Socrates, who said, "I cannot teach anybody anything. I can only teach them to think."

Chapter 1: Analyze

*No way of thinking or doing, however ancient, can
be trusted without proof.*

—Henry David Thoreau

Marybelle wasn't too sure. The last time Sammy had invited her out, they had ended up at a party she knew would infuriate her mother. Most of the kids there were seniors. There had been no parents present, and she thought she smelled marijuana. Sammy told her not to worry. Marybelle's best friend said the same thing and added that her parents would never find out and that she should stop worrying and just have some fun. The more her friends talked, the higher Marybelle's antennae went. This sounded like one of those times that her mother had talked about. "When smoke smells funny, there's more than fire," her mom had said . . . more than once. "Just figure it out, and get out."

Critical thinking begins with the ability to analyze, the most prevalent thinking skill in the ELA standards. Analysis involves the tedious task of taking ideas and objects apart, looking carefully at the various components, and then reorganizing the ideas by the similarities and differences found. Analyzing is the opposite of synthesizing, the act of putting ideas together.

Analysis spills into many other thinking skills that require the parceling of information for the sake of clarity and understanding. This cognitive skill is inextricably linked to exercises in which similarities and differences are identified. For example, analysis is embedded in comparing and contrasting, classifying and sorting, discerning point of view and nuance, and prioritizing, sequencing, and delineating. Table 1.1 (page 16) provides examples of what this thinking skill looks and sounds like in the classroom.

Table 1.1: Analyze Look-Fors and Sound Bites

Looks Like	Sounds Like
Students with their heads together, discussing a character's strengths and weaknesses Students highlighting parts of speech in text by underlining or using colored markers Students sorting songs into musical genres with labeled piles Students color-coding parts of speech	"This is one characteristic." "Here is an example of each quality." "This item belongs in this group." "There are forty units for each of the eight groups." "Let's take this apart, piece by piece."

Analysis may be the most valuable left-brain critical thinking skill for K–12 students. As Marybelle's story suggests, analysis is also a big deal when it comes to figuring out what's up with friends outside the school walls. Inside or outside of school, analysis—the ability to figure out situations, make sense of schoolwork, understand how little clues can solve big problems or ease big decisions—is a premier survival skill for today's young people.

Throughout their school experiences, students will be asked to perform rigorous analyses. In math, they will analyze data; in literature, they will analyze setting, theme, character, motivation, and relationships to plot; in chemistry, they will analyze soil; and in the visual arts, they will analyze a painter's style. As they move out into the job world, they will analyze a financial statement, a political candidate's position, or a complex health-care statement.

Analysis is one of the basics in the thinking process. Unless it is done well, what follows as new learning will be flawed. In this sense, then, analysis is like the start of a race. The better the runner is able to get ready and get set, the better will be his or her start.

Examples From the CCSS: Analyze

Phonics and Word Recognition: RF.4.3. Know and apply grade-level phonics and word analysis skills in decoding words.

Key Ideas and Details: RL.8.1. Cite the textual evidence that most strongly supports an analysis of what the text says explicitly as well as inferences drawn from the text.

TALK THROUGH · Explicit Teaching Lesson

In the Talk-Through, phase I, the educator teaches the thinking skill explicitly. There are several elements to aid the teacher in this phase: motivational mindset, order of operations, instructional strategy, assessment, and metacognitive reflection.

To *analyze* is to separate any material or abstract entity into its constituent elements. Related terms include *diagnose, examine, classify, differentiate,* and *distinguish.*

Motivational Mindset

To begin the lesson on the skill *analyze*, hook learners by staging a taste test between two brands: for example, Coke and Pepsi (or two kinds of gum, cough drops, or toothpaste). This is a learner-friendly, high-energy exercise that will engage students and encourage them to begin to think about analysis.

Order of Operations

When analyzing something—whether it is a complex character in a novel, the chemicals that compose a compound, or the causes of a global event—the steps are the same. PART is an acronym used to help students learn this process:

Preview the whole situation.

Assess similarities and differences.

Reorganize by these similarities and differences.

Turn the analysis into a summary or synthesis.

First, analysis calls for a preview of the whole, a global look at the entire situation or circumstance, taking in as much information as possible. For example, if students are analyzing the elements of a culture in world history, they will preview the related chapter in the textbook. The next step is to assess the obvious parts, elements, or components. Students will find the attributes of a culture, such as how it is ruled, what the people do, how they survive, and so on. Next, students reorganize the information by labeling the parts: government, aesthetics, regional resources, and such. Finally, they turn the analysis of the parts into a succinct summary of facts. In effect, the analysis of how things are alike and different, the actual separation of parts, results in a synthesis.

Instructional Strategy

An effective strategy to teach the skill of analyzing explicitly is the fishbone diagram. W. Edwards Deming (1982) referenced this tool as a part of formal brainstorming;

management could use this tool to analyze components that are needed in attaining goals. The fishbone is a graphic that allows participants to sort out the parts of a bigger idea into headings, subheadings, and details. Figure 1.1 is a completed fishbone diagram on an English literature theme: the American Dream.

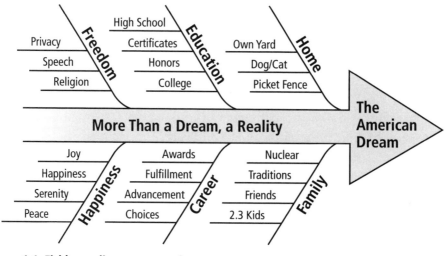

Figure 1.1: Fishbone diagram example.

Select a topic or concept that is appropriate for your subject area, and guide the students through the process of analyzing the key parts, subheads, and details using the fishbone diagram in appendix A on page 188. Visit **go.solution-tree.com /commoncore** to download the reproducibles in this book. These elements are called the head of the fish (target idea), the ribs (subheads), the riblets (details), and the spine (underlying theme).

Assessment

To check for students' understanding of how to use the skill, ask them to complete one of the following three assessments:

1. What data did you use from the text to show the cause-and-effect relationships you diagrammed?

2. Explain why the big-idea themes that thread the content of the current study unit are important to the unit.

3. Analyze your own health and wellness using a fishbone diagram.

Metacognitive Reflection

To promote students' thinking about analysis, divide the students into teams, and ask them to discuss how often they use the skill of analyzing and whether PART needs to be tweaked for clarity.

WALK THROUGH

Classroom Content Lesson

In the Walk-Through, phase II, teachers practice the thinking skill within content-based lessons, providing guidance to ensure the proper application of the skill. ELA Standard 10 recommends literature and instructional texts that are available for coupling with grade-level lessons.

▶ Elementary Level

Read aloud a grade-level story recommended by Standard 10. Ask the students to brainstorm the events of the story. Pick ten to fifteen events from the list, and invite groups to each sketch a fishbone on an 8 × 10 newsprint sheet or overhead slide. Ask one group to come forward and tape its sketch on the board for all to see or use the SMART Board to project the slide. Have a group discussion about the display.

▶▶ Middle Level

Present a fishbone diagram to the class. Using a current event, walk the students through filling out the diagram to show the causes of the event.

Assign students to organize themselves into cooperative groups of three. Give each group markers and a large sheet of newsprint on which to create a fishbone diagram. Help them find magazines or newspapers with stories they can analyze for cause and effect. At the end, allow a carousel hunt around the room so all can see. For the hunt, invite the teams to post their completed posters on the classroom walls. With one team member staying by the poster to answer questions, the others take a spin around the classroom, moving from poster to poster at your signal. They can ask questions, give constructive feedback, or discuss the poster's content.

▶▶▶ Secondary Level

Ask students to participate in a think-pair-share to determine what strategies are most important when making a proof for an isosceles triangle. Have the students discuss and narrow the list to three, such as: (1) review theorems and postulates, (2) review the properties of lines, angles, and triangles, and (3) establish the logical progressions. Assign a common problem for the pairs to solve with the three strategies. Ask matched pairs to review others' ideas and to generate a discussion for the whole class.

DRIVE THROUGH

CCSS Performance Task Lesson

During the Drive-Through, phase III, the thinking skill is transferred to authentic applications using CCSS performance tasks, allowing educators to make a direct connection between the selected thinking skill and the new standards. To deepen students' confidence with this skill, the teacher facilitates the student work, moving the students closer and closer to independent practice. Once the students are able to employ the skill independently, they are ready to transfer it across the curriculum. (For additional performance tasks, browse Common Core State Standards, Performance Tasks, Appendix B [NGA & CCSSO, 2010b].)

▶ Elementary Level

The following sample performance task illustrates the application of the ELA standard RL.4.5 (Reading: Literature, grade 4, standard 5):

> Students *refer to the structural elements (e.g., verse, rhythm, meter) of* Ernest Lawrence Thayer's "Casey at the Bat" when analyzing the *poem* and contrasting the impact and *differences* of those *elements* to a *prose* summary of the *poem.* (NGA & CCSSO, 2010b, p. 70)

▶▶ Middle Level

The following sample performance task illustrates the application of the ELA standard RI.6.3 (Reading: Informational Text, grade 6, standard 3):

> Students *analyze in detail how* the early years of Harriet Tubman (as related by author Ann Petry) contributed to her later becoming a conductor on the Underground Railroad, attending to how the author *introduces, illustrates, and elaborates* upon the events in Tubman's life. (NGA & CCSSO, 2010b, p. 93)

▶▶▶ Secondary Level

The following sample performance task illustrates the application of the ELA standard RST.9–10.1 (Science & Technical Subjects, grades 9–10, standard 1):

> Students *cite specific textual evidence* from Annie J. Cannon's "Classifying the Stars" to *support* their *analysis* of the scientific importance of the discovery that light is composed of many colors. Students *include* in their *analysis precise details* from the text (such as Cannon's repeated use of the image of the rainbow) to buttress their explanation. (NGA & CCSSO, 2010b, p. 138)

Reflection Questions

These questions are designed to enrich your learning from doing. Such reflection enables you to deepen your understanding of the lessons you have just provided.

You might also consider modifying these questions to further guide your students' reflection on this thinking skill.

1. How does the skill of analyzing connect to something you already do in your classroom?

2. How might you integrate this skill more explicitly in your lessons?

3. What is the most helpful takeaway concerning this critical thinking skill?

4. What will you do to help students become better with this skill? Be specific.

5. How might you "take apart" or "analyze" the Common Core State Standards? Where would you start? What questions and criteria would you have to consider before attempting the task?

Chapter 2: Evaluate

It is the mark of an educated mind to be able to
entertain a thought without accepting it.

—Aristotle

"Mom," Jaime started. "I've got a question for you. Why does that man on the news keep saying that Mexico is a bad place?"

"Just because somebody says something like that doesn't mean they are right. You have to evaluate what they are saying."

"And how do I do that? I don't know what *evaluating* means."

"It means you must ask them to show you proof for what they are saying. What are their facts? Then you balance those facts against facts from the other side. When you look at both sides and think about the facts, you are evaluating. So what facts do you know about Mexico that would give a different side?"

Evaluation is the complex mental act of placing a value on the nature, character, or quality of a person, object, event, concept, theory, or practice. It is a judgment, a weighing of the value. Evaluating is critiquing an essay, scoring a math test, judging a contest, appraising a project, assigning a grade, or determining worth.

It sounds so simple and straightforward, yet evaluation is a complicated process that, at best, involves making an assessment against a set of given criteria and assigning a value based on how well the object or action measures up. Evaluation is the final stop in the critical thinking process, although it may also be necessary throughout the process as it calls on analysis and synthesis, comparison and contrast to help determine the end's worth.

Table 2.1 provides examples of what this thinking skill looks and sounds like in the classroom.

Table 2.1: Evaluate Look-Fors and Sound Bites

Looks Like	Sounds Like
Students peer editing written work Students critiquing a presentation with a checklist Students holding scores up, using a scale of one through ten	"That's an A paper." "A flawless paper! Nothing to edit." "I like the precision of the work." "Here is my evidence." "Judging the winner was difficult because . . ."

Evaluation is a thought process that students and adults are required to exercise over and over on a daily basis. How skillfully the process is employed determines how well problems are solved. In this information-laden world, every citizen is faced with the challenge of hearing diverse ideas, theories, and opinions and making sound judgments regarding whether the information they are receiving is valid and reliable. Are the facts straight? Is there bias hidden in the writer's or newscaster's point of view? How trustworthy are the sources?

The strongest rationale for building the skill of evaluation may be its value outside the classroom, when students must assess misinformation that can bring harm. However, that position would unfairly limit the value of evaluation in schoolwork, family life, and careers. Every time a problem arises in an individual's life, that person must use evaluation skills to solve the problem. Some decisions in the real world are light and easily managed. What do we eat for dinner tonight? What shirt and tie combine well? What transportation should I use? Other evaluations help resolve more serious problems. Should I look for a new position more in line with my skills and preferences? Should I ask her to marry me? Should we have a third child? How am I going to care for my aging parents?

In school settings, both simple and complex problems require evaluation and judgment. Simple problems involve finding the conflict in a novel or replicating an experiment in the lab. More complexity is involved when selecting the best strategy for evaluating a persuasive speech. In all instances, however, evaluation is a prime skill to master in pursuit of critical thinking and in responding to many of the Common Core State Standards.

Examples From the CCSS: Evaluate

Integration of Knowledge and Ideas: RH.11–12.8. Evaluate an author's premises, claims, and evidence by corroborating or challenging them with other information.

Integration of Knowledge: RL.11–12.7. Analyze multiple interpretations of a story, drama, or poem (e.g., recorded or live production of a play or recorded novel or poetry), evaluating how each version interprets the source text. (Include at least one play by Shakespeare and one play by an American dramatist.)

TALK Explicit Teaching Lesson

THROUGH

In the Talk-Through, phase I, the educator teaches the thinking skill explicitly. There are several elements to aid the teacher in this phase: motivational mindset, order of operations, instructional strategy, assessment, and metacognitive reflection.

To *evaluate* is to determine or set the value or amount of an object or action. Related terms include *judge, calculate, compute, measure, audit, appraise, examine, inspect,* and *review.*

Motivational Mindset

To begin the lesson on the skill *evaluate,* hook the students by asking them to evaluate a recent activity completed (for example, an essay, an art project, a lab experiment) using a scale of one to ten. They should use three criteria of their choosing. Provide options for them to consider, such as: content, presentation, effectiveness, clarity, application, relevance, length, and examples. Students are to complete the evaluation and turn it in at the designated time. All submittals are anonymous.

Order of Operations

An evaluation begins with the essential criteria to be considered. Then the evidence is weighed against the criteria, and a judgment is made about how well the criteria are met. Finally, the total value is calculated and the final judgment given. This process is represented by the acronym JUDGE:

Justify essential criteria.

Use evidence to weigh against the criteria.

Decide how well the criteria are met.

Gather the sum total.

Express final judgment.

For example, a teacher assigns a persuasive essay using criteria developed with student input. The three critical criteria agreed upon are: (1) organization of logical argument, (2) evidence of persuasive language, and (3) reaction of reader. When the finished essays are read, both the student and the teacher assign a score of one to five on the student's essay for each criterion. The final totals are computed prior to the teacher conducting a discussion about the importance of the criteria in making the assessments.

Instructional Strategy

An effective strategy for developing students' evaluation skills is to use a plus/minus chart (see table 2.2 for an example) with a think-pair-share follow-up. After distributing the chart, allow time for the students to fill in the chart. Individually, students think about and evaluate the statements. Then ask the students to share their answers with a partner and note those opinions that don't match. Have the students discuss these and try to come to a common opinion before sampling ideas shared by pairs with the whole class.

Table 2.2: Plus/Minus Chart

Instructions: Evaluate statements by marking a (+) for those you agree with, a (-) for those you disagree with, and a (?) for those statements you are unsure of.	
Statement	**+ / − / ?**
1. The federal government has too many regulations.	
2. Banks need more freedom when deciding on credit card charges.	
3. Regulations protect consumers.	
4. When it comes to banking fees, it is best for the buyer to protect himself or herself.	
5. Big business needs more control for the good of the consumer.	
6. Consumer protection is a primary responsibility of the state governments.	
7. If the government had been on the ball, there would have been a collapse on Wall Street.	

Assessment

After hearing the different responses about the statements, invite the students to repeat a think-pair-share sequence to discuss the benefits of a plus/minus chart for evaluating a controversial topic.

Metacognitive Reflection

Close the discussion by asking students to reflect on what they have learned about making judgments from this lesson. What is the takeaway they can share with peers?

Classroom Content Lesson

In the Walk-Through, phase II, teachers practice the thinking skill within content-based lessons, providing guidance to ensure the proper application of the skill. ELA Standard 10 recommends literature and instructional texts that are available for coupling with grade-level lessons.

▶ Elementary Level

Select three poems (examples can be found in the CCSS, Appendix B, p. 17 [NGA & CCSSO, 2010b]). Project the titles on the SMART Board or screen and read the poems. Ask each student pair to choose the poem they like best and write down the reasons for their evaluation. Provide the pairs with a copy of a ranking ladder (a blank ranking ladder can be found in appendix A on page 189), and ask them to rank-order their top three reasons. Select two to four groups at random to show and discuss their ranking ladders. Give feedback to refine their thinking.

▶▶ Middle Level

For this lesson, use cooperative groups of three to review JUDGE before setting up the criteria for what defines acceptable and unacceptable text messages with friends. After students have defined the criteria, ask them to use these criteria to evaluate specific texting behaviors and place each criterion on the appropriate side of a scale. To conclude, ask each group to come up with a single text message about what they learned about evaluating text messages.

▶▶▶ Secondary Level

In this sample lesson, invite the class to brainstorm with a web or concept map how to evaluate the accuracy of data used by an author. After students read a selected nonfiction book, have them use the criteria to judge the author's data use. Ask students in cooperative groups of five to examine assigned chapters, especially noting the author's use of language and facts. Allow each group to present its findings prior to a final assessment of the book's accurate or inaccurate use of data. Conclude with a review of the essential criteria for making literary judgments.

DRIVE CCSS Performance Task Lesson

THROUGH

During the Drive-Through, phase III, the thinking skill is transferred to authentic applications using CCSS performance tasks, allowing educators to make a direct connection between the selected thinking skill and the new standards. To deepen students' confidence with this skill, the teacher facilitates the student work, moving the students closer and closer to independent practice. Once the students are able to employ the skill independently, they are ready to transfer it across the curriculum. (For additional performance tasks, browse Common Core State Standards, Performance Tasks, Appendix B [NGA & CCSSO, 2010b].)

▶ Elementary Level

The following sample performance task illustrates the application of the ELA standard RI.3.5 (Reading: Informational Text, grade 3, standard 5):

> Students use *text features*, such as the table of contents and headers, found in Aliki's text *Ah, Music!* to identify relevant sections and *locate information relevant to a given topic* (e.g., rhythm, instruments, harmony) *quickly and efficiently.* (NGA & CCSSO, 2010b, p. 61)

▶▶ Middle Level

The following sample performance task illustrates the application of the ELA standard RH.6–8.6 (History/Social Studies, grades 6–8, standard 6):

> Students evaluate Jim Murphy's *The Great Fire* to *identify* which *aspects of* the *text* (e.g., *loaded language* and the *inclusion of particular facts*) *reveal* his purpose; presenting Chicago as a city that was "ready to burn." (NGA & CCSSO, 2010b, p. 100)

▶▶▶ Secondary Level

The following sample performance task illustrates the application of the ELA standard RH.11–12.8 (History/Social Studies, grades 11–12, standard 8):

> Students *evaluate* the *premises* of James M. McPherson's argument regarding why Northern soldiers fought in the Civil War by *corroborating* the *evidence* provided from the letters and diaries of these soldiers with *other* primary and secondary *sources*

and *challenging* McPherson's *claims* where appropriate. (NGA &
CCSSO, 2010b, p. 183)

Reflection Questions

These questions are designed to enrich your learning from doing. Such reflection enables you to deepen your understanding of the lessons you have just provided. You might also consider modifying these questions to further guide your students' reflection on this thinking skill.

1. What judgment did you make today that had little impact on your day?

2. What judgment did you make today that was very important?

3. Use a plus/minus chart to evaluate your performance on a specific challenging task you completed recently (tax preparation, vacation planning, family budget), using three criteria of your choosing. How effective was your criteria, and how might you improve it?

4. When evaluating your own teaching effectiveness, what evidence do you consider to be the most accurate data: summative (test scores) or qualitative (student behavior, peer reviews, parent comments)?

Chapter 3: Problem Solve

It's not that I'm so smart, it's just that I stay with problems longer.

—Albert Einstein

"Mosquitoes," the doctor said. "Mosquitoes."

"But how can a mosquito make a whole village sick? This week, four children in our village died."

"You live next to a swamp. The water is bad. That is a big challenge. We must find a way to safeguard the people."

"Yes, I understand the urgency. But is it the mosquitoes or the bad water? Don't we have to attack both problems at once?"

"Both solutions are too costly for us. We have to find a simpler solution."

In Africa, mosquitoes are a major health threat. There is no money for fancy sprays or poisons as used in the Western world. This large, complex problem has befuddled the world health community. Finally, an affordable solution has been found. Simple cotton netting put over beds at night protects the villagers when they are most vulnerable.

Problem solving asks the thinker to employ several less-complex skills, including such critical thinking skills as analysis and evaluation, as part of the process. Problem solvers also may rely on the other side of the cognitive coin, calling on creative thinking skills to help solve a problem or create innovative solutions to meet a challenge that seems overwhelming.

Problem solving comes in two versions: messy and clean. Messy (often called ill-defined) problems are authentic, real-world, multidimensional issues that can have many different valid solutions; they present challenges that are difficult to define. Clean (often called well-defined) problems are those that can follow a set formula or a sequence of exact procedures to reach a solution. Following is an example of each:

- Clean—Two trains are speeding at each other with given speeds of 78 mph on the same track. They are 12 miles apart at 12 p.m. At what time will they collide?

- Messy—Mary hits her forehead with a whack. "OMG!" she texts her friend Kay. "What am I going to do? I've got two dates tonight. One for the prom and the other for the Bulls' game. I totally forgot. I just got flowers from both. These guys are really hot. OMG. Help! This is such a mess."

Table 3.1 provides examples of what problem solving looks and sounds like in the classroom.

Table 3.1: Problem Solve Look-Fors and Sound Bites

Looks Like	Sounds Like
Students with their heads together in groups	"What is the problem?"
Students using measurement tools	"How do we define this problem?"
Students using problem-solving graphic organizers	"What other ideas do you have?"
Students using decision-making graphic organizers	"Do we have accurate data?"
Students completing T-charts	"Is our data sufficient? Reliable?"

Life is filled with challenges and problems. As children grow older, they rely less on others to solve their problems. Gradually, they become independent problem solvers who can get dressed, get to school, finish homework, and do their chores. Their problems become more complex, and they become aware of more and more challenges and problems that are out of their control—for example, water pollution, poverty, and wars in many lands.

When problems get to a grand scale, another set of terms, *wicked* and *tame*, used by John Kao (2007), make a distinction based on complexity rather than clean and messy. Wicked problems are the larger and more complex of the messy problems. These attempt to address complex national or global issues, such as water conservation, health care, population migration, drug wars, and national security, that have no easy solutions.

Learning to solve different types of problems will contribute to students' success in different domains. Messy problems are usually associated with the arts, literature, and social sciences such as psychology and anthropology. They are also the most prevalent problems students face in their everyday lives dealing with people and situations outside the classroom. Clean problems are at home in science and mathematics. Sometimes a situation involves both clean and messy problems. For example, when a fire inspector is trying to find the cause of a fire, clean problems (mathematical formulas) may be part of a larger strategy to solve messy and wicked problems.

Students benefit most when learning about the problem-solving process enhances their dispositions about problem solving. Included among the characteristics needed for productive problem solving are risk taking, questioning assumptions, openness to ideas, willingness to connect divergent ideas, a respect for data, and attention to precision and accuracy.

Examples From the CCSS: Problem Solve

Integration of Knowledge and Ideas: RI.5.7. Draw on information from multiple print or digital sources, demonstrating the ability to locate an answer to a question quickly or to solve a problem efficiently.

Investigate Patterns: 8.SP.3. Use the equation of a linear model to solve problems in the context of bivariate measurement data, interpreting the slope and intercept. *For example, in a linear model for a biology experiment, interpret a slope of 1.5 cm/hr as meaning that an additional hour of sunlight each day is associated with an additional 1.5 cm in mature plant height.*

TALK Explicit Teaching Lesson

THROUGH

In the Talk-Through, phase I, the educator teaches the thinking skill explicitly. There are several elements to aid the teacher in this phase: motivational mindset, order of operations, instructional strategy, assessment, and metacognitive reflection.

Problem solving is one of the most desired skills of today's employers (American Management Association, 2010). To *problem solve* is to use cognitive processing to find a solution to a difficult question or situation. Related terms include *challenge, prove, analyze,* and *synthesize.*

Motivational Mindset

To create an effective hook for the explicit lesson about problem solving, give the students an interesting problem to solve. In this scenario, each pair of students takes a single piece of yarn and ties the ends to their right wrists. They repeat this with a second piece for the left wrists so that the yarn overlaps and creates an X between the two of them. The challenge is to separate from each other without untying the yarn.

Have the pairs list the steps they took to try to solve the problem. Do not provide a "right way" as you guide the closing dialogue. Instead, ask the students to focus on what they have learned about problem solving.

Order of Operations

The goal of this lesson is to learn how to solve any problem—clean or messy—with a reliable yet adaptable approach. While there are many kinds of specific problem-solving strategies—including the scientific method, particular methods for specific types of math problems, and resolution finding in literature and history—there are certain components that are embedded in all, as represented by the mnemonic SOLVE:

Select the problem.

Opt for a strategy.

Look for information.

Verify facts and data needed.

Express alternatives and selected solutions.

A sample problem to attend the explication of SOLVE focuses on students' tardiness to class. To determine how serious the problem is in their own class, the students choose to take a survey. Using SurveyMonkey (www.surveymonkey.com), the students provide information on how frequently they were late for class and how late they were. They ask the teacher to verify the data and then brainstorm strategies to diminish the tardiness.

Instructional Strategy

Work with the students to apply SOLVE to the following clean (table 3.2) and messy (table 3.3) problems.

Table 3.2: Clean Problem

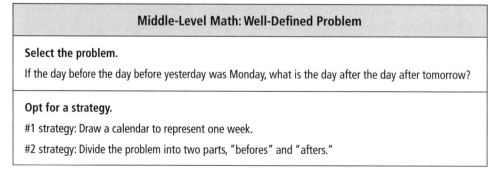

Middle-Level Math: Well-Defined Problem
Select the problem. If the day before the day before yesterday was Monday, what is the day after the day after tomorrow?
Opt for a strategy. #1 strategy: Draw a calendar to represent one week. #2 strategy: Divide the problem into two parts, "befores" and "afters."

Look for information.
#1 strategy: The day before the day before was Monday . . . mark the calendar, like a number line.
#2 strategy: Plot the "befores" and solve for the "afters."

Verify facts and data needed.
#1 strategy: Check the logic with a partner by talking through the problem.
#2 strategy: Check the facts for each part with another team. Show them your work.

Express alternatives and selected solutions.
#1 strategy: Best answer; only correct answer—(?)
#2 strategy: Answer solved—(?)

Once the students have completed these five steps, review the acronym's letters and key words. Encourage the students to store SOLVE in their journals or to make a poster.

Table 3.3: Messy Problem

Elementary-Level Social Studies: Bill of Rights
A recent locker search of all sixth graders has fueled a controversy about students' individual rights to privacy as guaranteed by the Constitution. The teacher uses this local incident to address the social studies lesson on the Bill of Rights.
Select the problem.   In groups of three, read the Bill of Rights, and apply your understanding to the recent locker searches. Were individual rights to privacy impinged upon? Why or why not? What is the evidence?
Opt for a strategy.   Use one of three options: 1. Create a graphic organizer depicting the gathered information and judgment.   2. Develop a script for a role play depicting an application of the Bill of Rights to the situation.   3. Present a persuasive speech advocating your point of view on this situation.
Look for information.   Show evidence from at least three resources, such as an article, blog, editorial, podcast, YouTube video, or interview.
Verify facts and data needed.   Cite all sources with publication, author, and date. Have a peer review the material and give you or your team feedback for needed revisions or blanket approval.
Express alternatives and selected solutions.   Present your findings and judgment with all necessary justification for your stand.

After this activity is finished, again return to SOLVE. Ask students to determine how helpful the mnemonic was as they went about solving the problem. Check for understanding and recall.

Assessment

Ask students to apply SOLVE to a real-world, ill-defined or messy problem. As a group, brainstorm a list of ill-defined problems. Have the students divide into collaborative groups of three and select one problem from the list. Make clear that they will use SOLVE as their guide for solving the problem and for determining how well they did. As each group presents its SOLVE to the entire class, the listening students use a SOLVE rubric you create to assess the performances.

Metacognitive Reflection

Ask students to first share a *highlight* (knowledge or information) about problem solving and then an *insight* (reflection or thought) about problem solving.

WALK THROUGH Classroom Content Lesson

In the Walk-Through, phase II, teachers practice the thinking skill within content-based lessons, providing guidance to ensure the proper application of the skill. ELA Standard 10 recommends literature and instructional texts that are available for coupling with grade-level lessons.

▶ Elementary Level

Select three clean problems from your curriculum. For example, use one-part/two-part problems in math or science questions about magnets, buoyancy, or living things. Guide the students through the SOLVE process with the first problem. Have them work as partners for the second selected problem. Ask several to share their thinking, and probe for clarity and reasons for using the acronym. Use the third problem to check for understanding and determine what formative feedback will help.

▶▶ Middle Level

Provide the students with a messy problem relevant to the grade. For example, "Some friends are cyberbullying your best friend, and you feel caught in the middle," or "You hate the sport that your dad most wants you to play, and it's time for try-outs." Model and label each of the steps of SOLVE before putting students into pairs. Encourage them to use and label SOLVE. Sample several ideas and probe the responses for clarity by asking students to provide facts or examples before giving each individual a messy problem to solve for homework.

▶▶▶ Secondary Level

Present a mixed clean and messy problem to students, or invite students to create their own. For example, "You have gotten a ticket for texting while driving that is a $100 fine or loss of license. Texting while driving is verboten in the family. It is also a family practice that any driving fines are entirely the responsibility of the guilty party. You are the designated driver to the prom, and you have promised a ride to your younger brother, who doesn't have a license." Divide students into pairs so they can collaborate on using SOLVE on this problem before sharing their solutions with another pair.

DRIVE CCSS Performance Task Lesson

THROUGH

During the Drive-Through, phase III, the thinking skill is transferred to authentic applications using CCSS performance tasks, allowing educators to make a direct connection between the selected thinking skill and the new standards. To deepen students' confidence with this skill, the teacher facilitates the student work, moving the students closer and closer to independent practice. Once the students are able to employ the skill independently, they are ready to transfer it across the curriculum. (For additional performance tasks, browse Common Core State Standards, Performance Tasks, Appendix B [NGA & CCSSO, 2010b].)

▶ Elementary Level

The following sample performance task illustrates the application of the Mathematics standard 2.MD.8 (Measurement and Data, grade 2, standard 8):

> Solve word problems involving dollar bills, quarters, dimes, nickels, and pennies, using $ and ¢ symbols appropriately. Example:
> If you have 2 dimes and 3 pennies, how many cents do you have?
> (NGA & CCSSO, 2010c, p. 20)

▶▶ Middle Level

The following sample performance task illustrates the application of the Mathematics standard 6.NS.8 (Number System, grade 6, standard 8).

> Solve real-world and mathematical problems by graphing points in all four quadrants of the coordinate plane. Include use of coordinates and absolute value to find distances between points with the same first coordinate or the same second coordinate. (NGA & CCSSO, 2010c, p. 43)

▶▶▶ Secondary Level

The following sample performance task illustrates the application of the ELA standard RH.11–12.7 (History/Social Studies, grades 11–12, standard 7):

> Students *integrate* the *information* provided by Mary C. Daly, vice president at the Federal Reserve Bank of San Francisco, with the data presented *visually* in the *FedViews* report. In their analysis of these *sources of information presented in diverse formats*, students frame and *address a question* or *solve a problem* raised by their *evaluation* of the evidence. (NGA & CCSSO, 2010b, p. 183)

Reflection Questions

These questions are designed to enrich your learning from doing. Such reflection enables you to deepen your understanding of the lessons you have just provided. You might also consider modifying these questions to further guide your students' reflection on this thinking skill.

1. Why would you introduce the skill of problem solving and the SOLVE process to students? How does this work with what you use now? Is it helpful? Why or why not?

2. How will you explicitly teach this skill? What topic can you use? Be as specific as possible.

3. What is your primary method for solving problems that arise in your own life?

Creative
Thinking

Embedded in the CCSS is the big idea of creativity and innovation. The associated thinking skills provide students with ways to demonstrate authentic evidence of what they have learned in any of the disciplines. Creativity taps into one's imagination and is often the magic link in problem solving and decision making because it brings to mind unusual, novel, and unique ideas. Creative thinking can be clever, wise, out-of-the-box thinking. It sometimes yields thoughts that seem outlandish, as the mind makes strange connections between ideas considered quite alien.

Innovation and creativity are inextricably linked. It has been said that innovation is imagination realized and that only when the creative thought is put into action does innovation occur. In the broadest sense, imagination, invention, and innovation are of the same ilk. They signal original, fluent, flexible, and elaborative thoughts (Torrance, 1974), and they are cornerstones of productive, generative thinking in the rich, rigorous, and relevant curriculum espoused in the CCSS. They are also necessary for effective problem solving, shrewd decision making, and productive ideation in the future world of our young citizens.

With that in mind, the skill set of creative thinking has been dissected into three skills that need explicit instruction with students across grade levels and content areas: (1) generate, (2) associate, and (3) hypothesize.

2

Chapter 4: Generate

The way to get good ideas is to get lots of ideas, and throw the bad ones away.

—Linus Pauling

———————————————

Emily, a first grader, epitomizes the youngster who is especially good at generating ideas. Every day, as the first graders enter the classroom, they are expected to go to the little table where the teacher is seated and tell her their "word of the day." It is the students' responsibility—in fact, their homework each night—to generate a word that they want to learn and work with the next day. Some kids are very slow to generate their words, but not Emily. Her fluency, flexibility, and originality are like ever-ready batteries. After all, she thinks like a scientist—an entomologist, to be specific, for she loves insects, bugs, creepy crawlies of all sorts and sizes. In the mornings, her words just flow from her: *caterpillar, butterfly, worm, garden snake, ladybug, jar, mosquito, microscope, meadow, net, tarantula,* and so on. Once she has her word written on the card, she is off to "study" her word in paint, sand, clay, or some other media on the choice board. Then the elaboration begins as she writes her daily sentences (story) around her pivot word.

Generating ideas is often the first step in producing a product or performing a presentation, both of which are considered evidence of learning. For example, the innovative production of a toy dragon using all six simple machines or the culminating statement that clearly persuades in a lively debate provides real evidence of understanding by the students involved. In both situations, the students need to generate many ideas to bring it all to fruition. This kind of creative and innovative thinking requires rigorous scaffolding in the classroom for students to become effective users of the skill. Table 4.1 provides examples of what generating ideas looks and sounds like in the classroom.

Table 4.1: Generate Look-Fors and Sound Bites

Looks Like	Sounds Like
Students creating a web, map, or list	"How about this . . ."
Students adding to a list of words	"Here's another crazy idea."
Students collaborating on the writing of lyrics	"Does this work?"
Students drawing lines to words that connect	"Great idea! Where did that come from?"
Students stringing ideas together	"Piggybacking on Joe's comment . . ."

Without skillfulness in readily generating a string of ideas, in all kinds of situations, students will lack an essential component in problem solving, decision making, and creative ideation. Brainstorming or generating ideas is a skill that can be explicitly learned with practice, rehearsal, and repetition. It is worth the effort as it is at the heart and soul of creative endeavors, big or small.

Examples From the CCSS: Generate

Text Types and Purposes: W.4.2. Write informative/explanatory texts to examine a topic and convey ideas and information clearly.

b. Develop the topic with facts, definitions, and details.

Research to Build and Present Knowledge: WHST.6–8.7. Conduct short research projects to answer a question (including a self-generated question), drawing on several sources and generating additional related, focused questions that allow for multiple avenues of exploration.

TALK THROUGH — Explicit Teaching Lesson

In the Talk-Through, phase I, the educator teaches the thinking skill explicitly. There are several elements to aid the teacher in this phase: motivational mindset, order of operations, instructional strategy, assessment, and metacognitive reflection.

Generate means to bring into existence. Related terms include *brainstorm*, *produce*, *develop*, *form*, *list*, and *create*.

Motivational Mindset

To grab students' interest, orchestrate a brief relay race. Depending on the focus, a timely topic is posted on the board. Possible generic topics are: government, scientific discoveries, literary genres, mathematical terms, healthy foods, figurative language devices, and sports.

Divide the class into teams of four to six, and begin the relay with two teams competing against each other for the longest list of synonyms or phrases associated with the topic or descriptions of the topic. The teams line up in front of the board. One member at a time goes to the board and adds to the list. That person then goes to the back of the line. Everyone on the team takes a turn adding to the brainstorming list. At the end of two minutes, the team with the most entries on the board is the winner. Then go to the next set of two teams, and finally have a playoff of the top two teams. Discuss the concept of generating ideas.

Order of Operations

To generate ideas, several mental operations must cause a FLOW:

First blast—call out a burst of ideas, connect to the topic.

Long list—add more words by associating and piggybacking on ideas.

Open mind—anything goes; defer judgment, go with the flow.

Work with the best—select the best idea, target the one with the most potential.

For example, when generating ideas for a science project, the students call out a first blast of ideas: simple machines and pendulums, electronics and robots, chemical compounds and reactions, and so on. Then by association and piggybacking on the growing list, new ideas emerge: piggybacking the electronics idea, electronic game boards, or piggybacking the simple machines idea, Rube Goldberg inventions. Keeping an open mind so that there are no censors, the listing continues: environmental studies, human life adaptations. Finally, the students begin to examine the list, looking for the best of the ideas. The idea that seems to have the widest appeal for creativity and uniqueness is the Rube Goldberg machines. Pairs could target a task for the machine to perform and create their version of a Rube Goldberg device to accomplish the goal. For example, a device could be designed to close the cupboard door or turn on the light.

Instructional Strategy

The four-fold concept development is a differentiation tool used to understand a concept or idea and is a great tool to introduce *generate*. Divide the students into teams, and provide each with a piece of poster paper. The students fold the poster paper into four corner sections. Then they make a small triangle fold with the folded corner. Once opened, this triangle fold appears as a diamond shape in which to write the focus word. Label the sections according to figure 4.1 (page 44). A blank four-fold concept development form can be found in appendix A on page 190. (Visit

go.solution-tree.com/commoncore to download the reproducibles in this book.)
Work with the students to develop the focus word by moving from one section to
the next in this order:

- List—the students brainstorm synonyms or ideas for the focus word.

- Rank—they look over the list and determine the top three words.

- Compare—they use the sentence "[Focus word] is like [concrete object]
  because both are: [They give three comparisons]."

- Illustrate—they draw a visual metaphor or picture of the object compared.

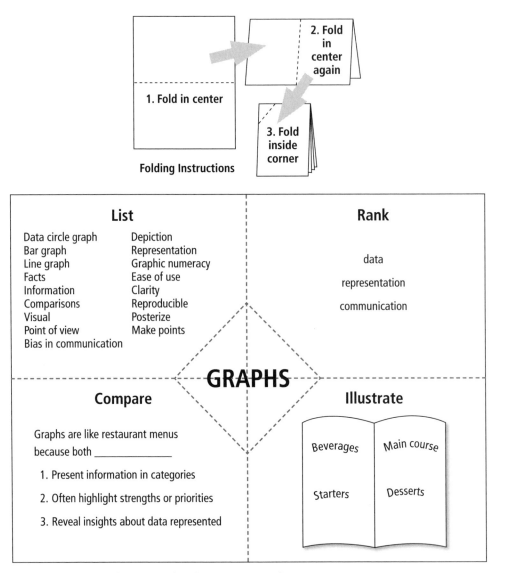

Figure 4.1: Four-fold concept development example.

Assessment

Ask the students to count the number of words generated on their lists for a fluency score. Award extra points for original or novel ideas that appear only on one chart in the room.

Metacognitive Reflection

Ask the students to consider the following questions:

- How many ideas can you come up with in three minutes?
- Do you consider yourself fluent in generating ideas?

WALK THROUGH   Classroom Content Lesson

In the Walk-Through, phase II, teachers practice the thinking skill within content-based lessons, providing guidance to ensure the proper application of the skill. ELA Standard 10 recommends literature and instructional texts that are available for coupling with grade-level lessons.

▶ Elementary Level

Ask students to generate word cards associated with a target word. For example, the target word might be *community*, *mammals*, *family*, or *addition*. Students generate as many cards as they can and post them on the wall randomly. Then, in teams of two, they arrange the words in alphabetical order. Finally, each looks over the entire list, selects one word, and makes a picture for the student-generated word wall.

▶▶ Middle Level

Ask the students to generate a web of green ideas for the community. Divide the students into groups of three, and instruct each group to choose one idea, research it, find a community agency to sponsor them or partner with them, and plan a service project to put into action.

▶▶▶ Secondary Level

Ask freshmen to list all the factors that impact student achievement. They should gather data on each factor, prioritize the factors by frequency or impact, and develop a student-friendly multimedia presentation to share with next year's incoming freshman class.

DRIVE CCSS Performance Task Lesson

THROUGH

During the Drive-Through, phase III, the thinking skill is transferred to authentic applications using CCSS performance tasks, allowing educators to make a direct connection between the selected thinking skill and the new standards. To deepen students' confidence with this skill, the teacher facilitates the student work, moving the students closer and closer to independent practice. Once the students are able to employ the skill independently, they are ready to transfer it across the curriculum. In each example, the skill *generate* is implied, not explicitly stated. (For additional performance tasks, browse Common Core State Standards, Performance Tasks, Appendix B [NGA & CCSSO, 2010b].)

▶ Elementary Level

The following sample performance task illustrates the application of the ELA standard RI.4.4 (Reading: Informational Text, grade 4, standard 4):

> Students *determine the meaning of domain-specific words or phrases*, such as *crust, mantle, magma*, and *lava*, and important *general academic words and phrases* that appear in Seymour Simon's *Volcanoes*. (NGA & CCSSO, 2010b, p. 76)

▶▶ Middle Level

The following sample performance task illustrates the application of the ELA standard RL.6.6 (Reading: Literature, grade 6, standard 6):

> Students *explain how* Sandra Cisneros's choice of words *develops the point of view of the* young *speaker in* her story "Eleven." (NGA & CCSSO, 2010b, p. 89)

▶▶▶ Secondary Level

The following sample performance task illustrates the application of the ELA Standard RI.11–12.9 (Reading: Informational Text, grades 11–12, standard 9):

> Students *analyze* Thomas Jefferson's Declaration of Independence, identifying its *purpose* and evaluating *rhetorical features* such as the listing of grievances. Students compare and contrast the *themes* and arguments found there to those of other *U.S. documents of historical and literary significance*, such as the Olive Branch Petition. (NGA & CCSSO, 2010b, p. 171)

Reflection Questions

These questions are designed to enrich your learning from doing. Such reflection enables you to deepen your understanding of the lessons you have just provided. You might also consider modifying these questions to further guide your students' reflection on this thinking skill.

1. How and when do you have students generate a long list of ideas?

2. Where are the opportunities in your subject matter for students to generate, produce, or make something as evidence of their learning?

3. What takeaway from this chapter will enhance a lesson or unit you are doing?

4. Complete the following sentence: It is easy for me to generate many ideas when I . . .

2

Chapter 5: Associate

Associate reverently, as much as you can, with your
loftiest thoughts.

—Henry David Thoreau

A youngster sees a seagull fly by in the summer sky, and his dad does what all parents do with their toddlers. He points to the seagull and says, "Bird."

The child mimics his dad and points and says, "Bird."

"Yes, that's a bird. A bird flies in the sky."

Suddenly, a butterfly floats down to land on the child's arm, and he says, "Bird."

To his surprise, his dad says, "No, that's a butterfly."

Then a plane soars overhead, and the little one, making a natural connection again, deliberately points to the sky and says, "Bird."

But again, much to the child's disappointment and confusion, his dad says, "No. That's an airplane."

To associate ideas is to piggyback on, connect, unite, combine, relate, and link different ideas to each other. It is creativity at work. Brainstorming, imagining, inventing, and innovating are evidence that the mind is making cognitive connections through association of thoughts. The result is a new concept or idea.

Table 5.1 (page 50) provides examples of what this thinking skill looks and sounds like in the classroom.

Table 5.1: Associate Look-Fors and Sound Bites

Looks Like	Sounds Like
Students reviewing and adding to a list of ideas	"That reminds me of . . ."
Students connecting words or phrases on paper	"Your word makes me think of . . ."
Students charting ideas on a flip chart	"Related to that idea is . . ."
Students noting ideas quickly	"What about the synonym . . ."
Partners alternating jotting down ideas	"I see another link between the . . ."

Concepts develop from a continued association process, as illustrated in the vignette opening this chapter. Children learn by associating one idea with another. They connect thoughts and then apply and generalize the ideas to build new concepts. Building concepts through critical associations is a trial-and-error process as the concept becomes more refined. This is how kids develop big, umbrella ideas about the world around them.

While it is a creative skill, associating ideas is also a critical skill in discerning similarities and differences. Learning how to identify associated types of problems in math, to link cause with effect in the science lab, and to relate symptoms to an illness in the real world makes association a most worthy higher-order thinking skill for 21st century thinking.

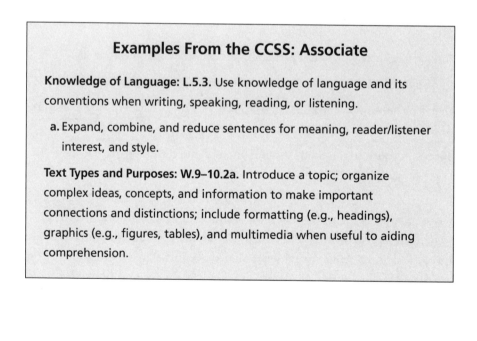

Examples From the CCSS: Associate

Knowledge of Language: L.5.3. Use knowledge of language and its conventions when writing, speaking, reading, or listening.

a. Expand, combine, and reduce sentences for meaning, reader/listener interest, and style.

Text Types and Purposes: W.9–10.2a. Introduce a topic; organize complex ideas, concepts, and information to make important connections and distinctions; include formatting (e.g., headings), graphics (e.g., figures, tables), and multimedia when useful to aiding comprehension.

TALK Explicit Teaching Lesson

THROUGH

In the Talk-Through, phase I, the educator teaches the thinking skill explicitly. There are several elements to aid the teacher in this phase: motivational mindset, order of operations, instructional strategy, assessment, and metacognitive reflection.

To *associate* is to connect or bring together into relationship. Related terms include *unite, link, combine, align,* and *relate.*

Motivational Mindset

To introduce the skill of associating ideas, test students' familiarity with the grocery store. Ask students to write down the name of the aisle in which particular products are found and to hold up their responses. For example, ask students to name the aisle in which they might find toothpicks. Once everyone has held up a response, discuss the results. Then ask students to explain what associations they made in making their decision. Repeat the exercise with other items that may be difficult to locate, such as sliced almonds, popcorn, paper plates, and so on.

Order of Operations

Associating ideas often starts with a visual or mental scan of previously noted ideas. The brain literally makes a dendritic connection between ideas that are related. It is important at this point in the association process to just play along and not censor anything. Allow all ideas to flow. Anything goes. Review the list again to see if anything sparks; it is important to allow time for the piggybacking to take place. When the ideas have been exhausted, review the list and keep the best ideas for development. This process can be summed up with SPARK:

Scan the list of ideas for associations.

Play along with connections made.

Allow anything.

Review again for more related ideas.

Keep the best for development.

A simple example is the formal brainstorming process. A middle school class is brainstorming ideas for fund-raising for a field trip to Springfield, Illinois, to visit the capitol. Ideas come fast and furious: spaghetti dinner, car wash, candy sale, tickets to a play, a newspaper to distribute at a cost. Then there is a long pause as the entire class scans the list. Finally, someone makes a connection and says, "I'm going to piggyback on Shawn's idea about the car wash. How about offering yard work for

2

the neighborhood? It's spring, and there are always yard cleanup jobs." Others jump in and add ideas: babysitting, dog walking, errands, and all kinds of neighborhood services.

"Yeah! What if we create a brochure of things we can do?"

"I love that idea."

"We could call it, 'Spring Into Spring With Springfield Services.'"

Instructional Strategy

ABC graffiti is an activity that requires the skill of associating. Essentially, the alphabet becomes an advance organizer for the creative process. In figure 5.1, the target focus is Word War II. Teams work on their own poster paper using specific colored markers to designate their team. In three minutes, they have to fill in one idea or association for each letter of the alphabet. After three minutes, they have one minute to go around to the other teams' posters to add new words using their own team colors. In the end, each team can see, because of the color coding, how many associations they have made beyond their initial efforts. Students can review and compare with the SPARK process. A blank ABC graffiti chart can be found in appendix A on page 191.

World War II

A	N
B	O
C	Pearl Harbor
D-Day	Q
E	Roosevelt
F	S
G	T
H	U
I	V
J	W
K	X
L	Y
M	Z

Figure 5.1: ABC graffiti example.

Assessment

Each team counts the number of entries on all of the papers in the room, scoring their results: two points for words on their own paper and five points for words on other teams' papers. More value is placed on associations beyond the original or first idea.

Metacognitive Reflection

Each team, using the SPARK order of operations, comes up with three possible ways that this strategy could be adapted using online technology.

WALK

THROUGH

Classroom Content Lesson

In the Walk-Through, phase II, teachers practice the thinking skill within content-based lessons, providing guidance to ensure the proper application of the skill. ELA Standard 10 recommends literature and instructional texts that are available for coupling with grade-level lessons.

▶ Elementary Level

Work with the students to fill in an ABC graffiti chart. This can be used for any content area. For instance, students can use their prior knowledge to contribute to an ABC graffiti exercise on the topic of the Civil War or the branches of government in social studies class. They can use the ABC graffiti exercise in science class to unpack and classify living things or in math to examine strategies for the calculation of problems.

▶▶ Middle Level

Complete an ABC graffiti chart with students about a current topic of study. Then have student teams delve into their textbooks to compare the information found there with what they have listed on the chart. The goal is to list as many ideas outside of the textbook as possible.

▶▶▶ Secondary Level

Associating ideas using an ABC graffiti activity is useful for juniors and seniors in exploring career options or to investigate options for college. Work with students to create an ABC graffiti chart of the most interesting career choices. Consider displaying the completed chart in the guidance office to spur the imagination of all high school students.

DRIVE CCSS Performance Task Lesson

THROUGH

During the Drive-Through, phase III, the thinking skill is transferred to authentic applications using CCSS performance tasks, allowing educators to make a direct connection between the selected thinking skill and the new standards. To deepen students' confidence with this skill, the teacher facilitates the student work, moving the students closer and closer to independent practice. Once the students are able to employ the skill independently, they are ready to transfer it across the curriculum. (For additional performance tasks, browse Common Core State Standards, Performance Tasks, Appendix B [NGA & CCSSO, 2010b].)

▶ Elementary Level

The following sample performance task illustrates the application of the ELA standard RL.4.7 (Reading: Literature, grade 4, standard 7):

> Students *make connections between the visual presentation* of John Tenniel's illustrations *in* Lewis Carroll's *Alice's Adventures in Wonderland* and the text of the story to *identify* how the pictures of Alice reflect *specific descriptions* of her *in the text.* (NGA & CCSSO, 2010b, p. 70)

▶▶ Middle Level

The following sample performance task illustrates the application of the ELA standard RL.8.2 (Reading: Literature, grade 8, standard 2):

> Students *summarize the development* of the morality of Tom Sawyer in Mark Twain's novel of the same name and analyze its connection to themes of accountability and authenticity by noting how it is conveyed *through characters, setting, and plot.* (NGA & CCSSO, 2010b, p. 89)

▶▶▶ Secondary Level

The following sample performance task illustrates the application of the ELA standard RL.9–10.2 (Reading: Literature, grades 9–10, standard 2):

> Students *analyze in detail the theme* of relationships between mothers and daughters and how that *theme develops over the course of* Amy Tan's *The Joy Luck Club.* Students search the text for *specific details* that show how the *theme emerges* and *how it is shaped and refined* over the course of the novel. (NGA & CCSSO, 2010b, p. 121)

Reflection Questions

These questions are designed to enrich your learning from doing. Such reflection enables you to deepen your understanding of the lessons you have just provided. You might also consider modifying these questions to further guide your students' reflection on this thinking skill.

1. How might you use ABC graffiti to explicitly teach students how to use the SPARK process to associate ideas when doing projects and tasks that require the creative flow of ideas and information?

2. Do you agree or disagree that associating ideas is so intuitive that students attribute their ability to make connections to innate gifts and not to a learned skill? Justify your thinking.

3. What connections can you make between the explicit teaching of thinking skills and the goal of the Common Core State Standards to have every student career and college ready?

Chapter 6: Hypothesize

The great tragedy of science is the slaying of a beautiful hypothesis by an ugly fact.

—Thomas Huxley

For their final performance assessment, students, working in teams of four, were required to present their findings on the theory of why the dinosaurs became extinct. As each team took a turn, the speaker for the group stood proudly; showed the graphs, pictures, and research; and reported the hypothesis they had adopted. One hypothesis put forth was this: "It's only a working theory, but we think the reason the dinosaurs disappeared from the earth is because of the Ice Age that descended upon them. It wiped them out because there was no vegetation left for them to eat and survive."

In the school setting, the thinking skill of hypothesizing may take on a weighty cognitive role. It may be part of the formal scientific method seen in biology class; it may be found in the plot predictions made by English literature students as they read a novel; or it could even be a part of the metacognitive thinking that students do as they are anticipating their grade on an essay in history class. Table 6.1 (page 58) provides examples of what hypothesizing looks and sounds like in the classroom.

It is not surprising that the higher-order thinking skill of hypothesizing is cited in the CCSS, as it appears in a number of high-yield instructional strategies (Costa & Kallick, 2000; Marzano, Pickering, & Pollock, 2001). Hypothesizing, guessing, and following hunches are natural thinking paths for learners as they generate creative ideas and produce, invent, and innovate. In fact, this is the skill of the scientist, as famously noted in the scientific method:

1. Ask a question.

2. Do background research.

3. Construct a hypothesis.

4. Test your hypothesis by doing an experiment.

5. Analyze your data and draw a conclusion.

6. Communicate your results. (Science Buddies, n.d.)

Making a hypothesis is a natural component of any kind of problem solving, whether it is in the classroom or in real-life situations. Imagine that you are driving along and sense that there is something wrong with the steering. Immediately you think about the tires. As you pull over, you are already hypothesizing about when, where, and how you might have gotten a flat. Was it when you drove through the alley to take a shortcut? Did you pick up a nail? Could it have been from the long trip to Indiana last weekend? It was so hot that you may have worn the tires down from the excessive heat. The guessing goes on until you finally get out and see the nail in the tire.

The refrigerator has spontaneously defrosted, and you find a puddle of water on the kitchen floor. You automatically start hypothesizing. Did the power go off? Did the motor burn out on this old fridge? Did you forget to close the freezer door? Or maybe you bumped the temperature control switch on the inside wall? After close inspection, your final hypothesis is that the refrigerator defrosted because the motor stopped working, as nothing will restart it.

Table 6.1: Hypothesize Look-Fors and Sound Bites

Looks Like	Sounds Like
Students estimating the distance objects will travel Students considering different possible stage directions Students sketching possible plans to build a project Students testing and measuring objects to see if they fit Students pausing over a palette of paints	"My best guess is . . ." "I think if we try it this way . . ." "I'm guessing . . ." "Let's assume for a minute that . . ." "What if we look at it another way?"

Hypothesizing is such a huge part of what we do in our daily lives. If students are to become effective, successful problem solvers in all aspects of their lives, they need to have a formal look at this important thinking skill.

Examples From the CCSS: Hypothesize

Statistics & Probability: S-ID.4. Use the mean and standard deviation of a data set to fit it to a normal distribution and to estimate population percentages. Recognize that there are data sets for which such a procedure is not appropriate. Use calculators, spreadsheets, and tables to estimate areas under the normal curve.

Statistics & Probability: 6.SP.1. Recognize a statistical question as one that anticipates variability in the data related to the question and accounts for it in the answers. *For example, "How old am I?" is not a statistical question, but "How old are the students in my school?" is a statistical question because one anticipates variability in students' ages.*

TALK THROUGH   Explicit Teaching Lesson

In the Talk-Through, phase I, the educator teaches the thinking skill explicitly. There are several elements to aid the teacher in this phase: motivational mindset, order of operations, instructional strategy, assessment, and metacognitive reflection.

To hypothesize means to believe enough to act, even though there is uncertain or tentative evidence. Related terms include *predict, develop, interpret, synthesize, estimate, anticipate, infer,* and *speculate.* Martin H. Fischer (n.d.) clarifies what a hypothesis is: "Don't confuse hypothesis and theory. The former is a possible explanation; the latter, the correct one. The establishment of theory is the very purpose of science."

Motivational Mindset

To spark students' interest and pique their curiosity, walk into the classroom with an empty box that is secured tightly, and place it front and center for all to see. Ask the students to discuss with a partner what they think is in the box. They should support their hypotheses with the facts that they are using to guess. Allow about three minutes for this discussion.

Ask the pairs to share some of their thoughts about the box and give their rationale for the hypotheses they offer. Now for the unveiling. Inside is an object that leads to the next mystery. What does this object have to do with what the students are going to learn? Continue the conversation until the students close in on the topic.

Depending on the topic, the box could hold a bone, a laptop computer, field glasses, anything that is somehow related to the topic. This exercise will make the students curious enough to start hypothesizing.

Order of Operations

To hypothesize is to question and connect. First, focus on the idea, then make mental connections, and finally, concretize the hunch or prediction by verbalizing it. The AHA acronym is appropriate here:

Ask questions about the target idea or situation.

Harbor conscious connections.

Announce the hunch, and try to confirm.

The act of generating a hypothesis is a skill that will serve students not only in school but also when they have left school and begun their careers. With reflective practice, students will be able to hone this skill so that a hunch becomes more than intuition but a cognitive strategy employable in a variety of situations.

Instructional Strategy

Poll Everywhere (www.polleverywhere.com) is a powerful software tool or app for handheld wireless devices (cell phones) or computers. Teachers can use this in the classroom to activate prior knowledge about the target concepts, skills, or topics. Questions are posed, and participants weigh in by voting online or via texting. They hypothesize or make predictions about an idea, and the results show up in graph format as a projected image. Questions can be posed in multiple-choice, true/false, and agree/disagree formats. Following are two examples:

1. Based on your experience, what is best way to end bullying in our school?
   - ▶ Tougher penalties for offenders
   - ▶ More security personnel in the hallways
   - ▶ Mandatory anti-bullying classes for everyone
   - ▶ Mediation between offender and victim
2. Good grades are the primary reason to go to school.
   - ▶ Agree
   - ▶ Disagree

When learners hypothesize and predict outcomes, their curiosity is piqued, and they are motivated to find the answers. They want to investigate to confirm or validate their thinking.

Assessment

Ask the students to create a "Prediction Page" to record their hypotheses of what might happen in their lives in the next month, by the end of the semester, and by the end of the year, and then verify them.

Metacognitive Reflection

Ask students to discuss why it is important to hone the skill of hypothesizing and how it may apply to their lives outside of school.

WALK THROUGH Classroom Content Lesson

In the Walk-Through, phase II, teachers practice the thinking skill within content-based lessons, providing guidance to ensure the proper application of the skill. ELA Standard 10 recommends literature and instructional texts that are available for coupling with grade-level lessons.

▶ Elementary Level

Bring in a large odd-shaped sack, and have the students guess what is in the sack by asking questions similar to those on the game show *21*. Students work in pairs, and they can offer a guess of what they think is in the sack only after they ask their question. Some pairs will ask their questions early; others will wait to hear the results of the other questions.

▶▶ Middle Level

Assign a short story, but do not provide the end. Have the students come up with possible endings to the story. Their hypotheses are graded on their logical incorporation of existing facts gleaned from the part of the story they read.

▶▶▶ Secondary Level

Ask students to respond to one of the following scenarios with an original hypothesis that is supported with a rationale. What if . . .

1. Germany had developed an atomic weapon and had won World War II?
2. Alcohol was illegal and marijuana was legal?
3. Seventy percent of elected officials in the United States were women and 30 percent were men?
4. Shakespeare was a modern-day author?
5. America had adopted the metric system in 1990?

DRIVE CCSS Performance Task Lesson

THROUGH

During the Drive-Through, phase III, the thinking skill is transferred to authentic applications using CCSS performance tasks, allowing educators to make a direct connection between the selected thinking skill and the new standards. To deepen students' confidence with this skill, the teacher facilitates the student work, moving the students closer and closer to independent practice. Once the students are able to employ the skill independently, they are ready to transfer it across the curriculum. In each example, the skill *hypothesize* is implied, not explicitly stated. (For additional performance tasks, browse Common Core State Standards, Performance Tasks, Appendix B [NGA & CCSSO, 2010b].)

▶ Elementary Level

The following sample performance task illustrates the application of the ELA standard RL.5.2 (Reading: Literature, grade 5, standard 2):

> Students *summarize* the plot of Antoine de Saint-Exupéry's *The Little Prince* and then reflect on the *challenges* facing the *characters in the story* while employing those and other *details in the text* to discuss the value of inquisitiveness and exploration as *a theme* of the *story*. (NGA & CCSSO, 2010b, p. 70)

▶▶ Middle Level

The following sample performance task illustrates the application of the ELA standard RST.6–8.9 (Science & Technical Subjects, grades 6–8, standard 9):

> Students construct a holistic picture of the history of Manhattan by *comparing and contrasting the information gained from* Donald Mackay's *The Building of Manhattan* with the *multimedia sources* available on the "Manhattan on the Web" portal hosted by the New York Public Library. (NGA & CCSSO, 2010b, p. 100)

▶▶▶ Secondary Level

The following sample performance task illustrates the application of the Mathematics standard S-MD.3 (High School: Statistics & Probability, Using Probability to Make Decisions, high school, standard 3):

> Develop a probability distribution for a random variable defined for a sample space in which theoretical probabilities can be calculated; find the expected value. *For example, find the theoretical probability distribution for the number of correct answers*

obtained by guessing on all five questions of a multiple-choice test where each question has four choices, and find the expected grade under various grading schemes. (NGA & CCSSO, 2010c, p. 83)

Reflection Questions

These questions are designed to enrich your learning from doing. Such reflection enables you to deepen your understanding of the lessons you have just provided. You might also consider modifying these questions to further guide your students' reflection on this thinking skill.

1. In your learning community, how might you focus on the skill of valuing hunches, generating hypotheses, predicting outcomes, and estimating results as part of your focus on student success?

2. How might you build one opportunity for hypothesizing into your lessons in math? Science? Social studies? Language arts? Technology?

3. Hypothesize the effects of the CCSS being implemented with fidelity throughout the United States. Compare your prediction with a colleague's.

Complex Thinking

The concept of complex thinking is complex in itself. Complexity involves the sophistication of the language used, including word choice and sentence structure, as well as the level of discipline-based concepts. With complex thinking, the student is expected to not only read with literal clarity but also to interpret what is implied. Complex thinking requires skill in determining the author's perspective and purpose, the inherent bias, the nuance of tone and tenor, and the real meaning of the words on the page as crafted by the author, with intended or unintended persuasion. Complex thinking can be seen as the ability to cut through the abstract ideas presented in order to discern them in concrete ways. It helps the student grasp the underlying meaning of the concept.

All too often, texts are complex in vocabulary and concepts, and students with little background knowledge are lost before they begin the comprehension process. When narrative or informational texts combine discipline-specific vocabulary, sophistication in structure, subtle tonality, dense meaning, and intentional nuance, they can create frustrating barriers to student understanding.

This proficiency includes three skills: (1) clarify, (2) interpret, and (3) determine. Each of these thinking skills is a tool to examine complex text in both narrative and informational sources.

Chapter 7: Clarify

Clarity is the counterbalance of profound thoughts.
—Marquis De Vauvenargues

A senior in high school, excited about the sciences and determined to go into the field of biochemistry, decided to talk to a neighborhood friend who had gotten an advanced degree in biochemistry. While they were talking, the graduate mentioned that he had done his dissertation on the topic of chemical bonding. Enthusiastically, the young friend asked, "Can I read it?"

"Wow! I would love that. No one has ever even asked me the title of my dissertation. Let me get it. You can take as long as you want with it."

The senior was eager and started reading as soon as he got home. After the first few pages, he realized that he was stumbling and sputtering his way through the text. He was surprised by the complexity of what he was trying to understand, including unknown words, confusing passages, and intricate diagrams.

Upon returning the tightly bound book to its owner, the high school student reluctantly confessed, "Quite honestly, I wasn't able to really grasp this. It is really complicated stuff."

"Hey, no worries. Of course it is tough to read at this point in your studies. That's why you're going to college. You need more background in this area. Your classes will be able to clarify all of this for you."

"Thanks for the encouraging words. I was feeling pretty stupid."

The skill of clarifying can involve a number of interwoven tasks, such as:

- Analyzing vocabulary
- Simplifying questions
- Illustrating with examples to explain a point
- Paraphrasing
- Referencing a relevant source
- Illuminating a significant phrase

As delineated in the CCSS, clarifying the meaning of complex text involves knowledge of three tiers of vocabulary: (1) everyday words, (2) words encountered most often in written work rather than spoken communications, and (3) words that are content specific to a discipline or area. In addition to clarifying for meaning, word choice and the tenor and tone of words may need clarification.

Clarifying also involves understanding complex sentence structure, compound sentences, adverbial phrases, parenthetical notations, and intricate, long, and meandering passages. Metaphorically, clarifying is running a fine-tooth comb through the passage to reveal tangles that need smoothing. Table 7.1 provides examples of what this thinking skill looks and sounds like in the classroom.

Table 7.1: Clarify Look-Fors and Sound Bites

Looks Like	Sounds Like
Students participating in peer editing	"Let me paraphrase."
Students revising their papers	"Let me say it in my words."
Students finding the precise word	"It may not be clear."
Students shortening a long sentence	"A better way to express this is . . ."
Students diagramming a sentence	"If I could clarify my statement . . ."

If there is one skill that serves as a foundation for many of the more sophisticated skills, such as making inferences and generalizing, it is this skill of clarifying. Clarifying an idea put forth in verbal or written form is the essence of understanding, comprehending, or making meaning. It is one of the most foundational steps in becoming a literate learner. Without the ability to clarify, to see clearly what is intended by the author, much communicated information becomes misconstrued. Clarifying is one of the most essential thinking skills for literacy and learning across all disciplines.

Examples From the CCSS: Clarify

Vocabulary Acquisition and Use: L.4.4. Determine or clarify the meaning of unknown and multiple-meaning words and phrases based on grade 4 reading and content, choosing flexibly from a range of strategies.

Text Types and Purposes: WHST.6–8.2c. Use appropriate and varied transitions to create cohesion and clarify the relationships among ideas and concepts.

TALK THROUGH   Explicit Teaching Lesson

In the Talk-Through, phase I, the educator teaches the thinking skill explicitly. There are several elements to aid the teacher in this phase: motivational mindset, order of operations, instructional strategy, assessment, and metacognitive reflection.

To *clarify* is to make something, such as an idea or statement, clear or intelligible. Related terms include *explain, illuminate, elucidate, make transparent, unpack,* and *tell.*

Motivational Mindset

To introduce the idea of clarifying, divide the students into pairs. Have them decide who is A and who is B. Assign A the role of illustrator, and assign B the role of communicator. The communicator uses a picture of an object (for example, a bike, backpack, or geometric figure) to give verbal instructions to the illustrator, who draws exactly what is being described. Then when the drawing is complete, the pairs compare the drawing with the original picture. They finish up by talking about what was and was not clear in the instructions. End the exercise with a brief comment on clarity and why clarifying is such an important skill in reading, writing, seeing, and listening.

Order of Operations

The skill of clarifying begins with a search for meaning, a crystal-clear understanding of what is being said or read. Then one expresses significant words or phrases in his or her own way. The final step is articulating the idea in its simplest terms to expose the essence of it. This process is represented with the acronym SEE:

Seek the meaning of words and phrases.

Express these in your own words.

Expose the essence of the idea in the simplest terms.

For example, students consider the following Joe Wayman (1980) quote:

> If words remain words and sit quietly on the page; if they remain nouns and verbs and adjectives, then we are truly blind. But if words seem to disappear and our innermost self begins to laugh and cry, to sing and dance and finally to fly . . . if we are transformed in all that we are, to a brand new world, then, and only then, can we READ. (p. 46)

The students first look at the words and phrases that seem important (*transformed, truly blind, innermost self*) and figure out what they are stating. Next, they paraphrase and express the meaning in their own words: *readers must be involved in the reading, not just word calling.* Finally, they expose the essence clearly, in the simplest terms, to bring a final clarity: *reading takes the reader to a new place in his or her mind.*

Instructional Strategy

Post the Preamble to the United States Constitution for all the students to see:

> We the people of the United States, in order to form a more perfect union, establish justice, insure domestic tranquility, provide for the common defense, promote the general welfare, and secure the blessings of liberty to ourselves, and our posterity, do ordain and establish this Constitution for the United States of America. (NGA & CCSSO, 2010b, p. 93)

Also post the following four instructions:

1. Select three vocabulary words to clarify.
2. Write a clarifying question about a confusing phrase.
3. Paraphrase the Preamble in your own words.
4. Give a clear, simple, in-a-nutshell summary of the Preamble.

Have each student fold a piece of paper into fourths and number the four corners, 1, 2, 3, 4, and write the corresponding instruction in the quadrant (see fig. 7.1). Divide the students into teams of four, and number off 1, 2, 3, 4 in each team. All students follow the instructions and write their responses in the corresponding quadrant. When finished, they tear the paper into the four sections and pass all of the responses to instruction 1 to number 1 in the group, all the answers to instruction 2 to number 2 in the group, and so on. Each student then prepares an oral summary of the four responses. A sharing-round follows, with a final debriefing of the activity (Pete & Fogarty, 2009).

1. Select three vocabulary words to clarify.	2. Write a clarifying question about a confusing phrase.
3. Paraphrase the Preamble in your own words.	4. Give a clear, simple, in-a-nutshell summary of the Preamble.

Figure 7.1: Example exercise for the skill of *clarify*.

Assessment

Have the students choose one phrase from the Preamble, for example, "insure domestic tranquility," "provide for the common defense," or "secure the blessing of liberty to ourselves," and explain its meaning and restate the phrase to make it clearer to contemporary readers.

Metacognitive Reflection

Ask the students to compare clarifying the Preamble as a small group to understanding it on their own.

WALK THROUGH Classroom Content Lesson

In the Walk-Through, phase II, teachers practice the thinking skill within content-based lessons, providing guidance to ensure the proper application of the skill. ELA Standard 10 recommends literature and instructional texts that are available for coupling with grade-level lessons.

▶ Elementary Level

Clarifying meaning can be done quite successfully through dialogue. Divide students into pairs, and have them play the game "tell and retell." Looking at a picture book, one student begins by telling the other student what is happening in the picture. Then the other student restates it in his or her own words. As the students work, monitor the activity and ask probing questions to help the students go beyond simple recall and realize the depth of clarification. This demonstrates to students that they can clarify the ideas they see, hear, or read by paraphrasing or stating the ideas in their own words. If they can say it, they own it! Then have the pairs practice with the same picture book, but this time, they will read a page or paragraph to play the game.

▶▶ Middle Level

Practice the skill of clarifying by using optical illusions to encourage students to look closely and examine the image for telling details. Optical illusions are highly motivational for teens, and they encourage participation because they are nonjudgmental. Use M.C. Escher's drawings or search "optical illusions" online for a wealth of resources that range in difficulty for age appropriateness. Use the experience to move to clarifying text as students read and notice clues and cues to the meaning.

▶▶▶ Secondary Level

Ask students to watch a political network commentator or to read a political blog with two opposing views clearly articulated. Then ask students to present in a brief essay or discussion a clarification of both views by sharing the meaning and the message. Have them include words and phrases that clarify how each commentator was able to communicate his or her point of view. Discuss and debrief.

DRIVE CCSS Performance Task Lesson

THROUGH

During the Drive-Through, phase III, the thinking skill is transferred to authentic applications using CCSS performance tasks, allowing educators to make a direct connection between the selected thinking skill and the new standards. To deepen students' confidence with this skill, the teacher facilitates student work, moving the students closer and closer to independent practice. Once the students are able to employ the skill independently, they are ready to transfer it across the curriculum. (For additional performance tasks, browse Common Core State Standards, Performance Tasks, Appendix B [NGA & CCSSO, 2010b].)

▶ Elementary Level

The following sample performance task illustrates the application of the ELA standard RL.2.5 (Reading: Literature, grade 2, standard 5):

> Students *describe the overall story structure* of *The Thirteen Clocks* by James Thurber, *describing how* the interactions of the characters of the Duke and Princess Saralinda *introduce the beginning of the story* and how the suspenseful plot comes to an *end. (NGA & CCSSO, 2010b, p. 53)

▶▶ Middle Level

The following sample performance task illustrates the application of the ELA standard RL.6.6 (Reading: Literature, grade 6, standard 6):

Students *explain how* Sandra Cisneros's choice of words *develops the point of view of the* young *speaker in* her story "Eleven." (NGA & CCSSO, 2010b, p. 89)

▶▶▶ Secondary Level

The following sample performance task illustrates the application of the ELA standard RL.11–12.7 (Reading: Literature, grades 11–12, standard 7):

Students compare two or more *recorded or live productions* of Arthur Miller's *Death of a Salesman* to the written text, *evaluating* how *each version interprets the source text* and debating which aspects of the enacted *interpretations* of the play best capture a particular character, scene, or theme. (NGA & CCSSO, 2010b, p. 163)

Reflection Questions

These questions are designed to enrich your learning from doing. Such reflection enables you to deepen your understanding of the lessons you have just provided. You might also consider modifying these questions to further guide your students' reflection on this thinking skill.

1. Where do you rank this thinking skill of clarifying in terms of urgency for your students in their reading and writing:

   _____ At the very top

   _____ Very high

   _____ In the middle

   _____ Not that high

   _____ Not that important

2. What habit of mind (Costa & Kallick, 2000) is most prevalent when clarifying ideas? Why?

   _____ Persistence

   _____ Tolerance for ambiguity

   _____ Precision and accuracy

3. Complete the following:

   ▶ My best strategy for clarifying text is . . .

   ▶ I like or don't like reading primary source text because . . .

Chapter 8: Interpret

Everyone is of course free to interpret the work in his own way. I think seeing a picture is one thing and interpreting it is another.

—Jasper Johns

An eight-year-old asked his mom a question: "When I was watching a rerun of the old *Mork & Mindy* show, Mom, Mork said that a traffic light has a green light that means go, a red light that means stop, and a yellow light that means step on the gas. Doesn't the yellow light mean slow down?"

His mom explained, "Yes, the yellow light means slow down, but Mork was interpreting what he had been observing. Sometimes drivers do step on the gas for a yellow light as they try to get through the light before it turns red. He said it as a playful joke on a comedy show. You misinterpreted what he meant."

"Oh, I get it. He was saying it as a joke."

"Yes, he described what he saw happening, but it was the opposite of what was supposed to be happening."

A sophisticated level of understanding complex text is interpreting the author's meaning using the text itself and peripheral information. Interpreting meaning is a personalized approach to the text and presumes that the reader's scrutiny is heightened and personal bias or point of view may influence that interpretation. Interpretation of complex works calls for a level of sophistication in "sensing" the meaning. It is not merely a literal summation of the words and syntax, but a rendering of the impression that is transmitted through the words and the syntax. It is this subtle but critical difference between clarifying and interpreting that makes the explicit teaching of the two skills essential.

For example, consider the phrase "That's great!" How would you interpret the meaning? Is it a positive assessment, or is it a sarcastic comment? Without a known context, the interpretation may vary. In addition, the level of cynicism of the reader may influence the interpretation, as one reader might assume a cynical viewpoint rather than a complimentary one.

Consider another example: "The contents of the will came as quite a surprise to the heirs gathered in the room." This sentence could be interpreted as a good thing or a bad thing based on past experiences of various readers. If their prior experience about the reading of a will has been primarily with diabolical mysteries in novels or television dramas, they may see this as a warning of ominous things to come. But if they have had a family experience of a surprise inheritance, they may interpret this line as a sign of wonderful news.

These examples illustrate the intricacies of interpreting what one reads or hears. On the surface, it seems clear, but with nuance and innumerable extenuating circumstances, a more involved interpretation takes shape.

Table 8.1 provides examples of what this thinking skill looks and sounds like in the classroom.

Table 8.1: Interpret Look-Fors and Sound Bites

Looks Like	Sounds Like
Students collaborating with a peer	"Their performance was insightful."
Students changing symbols to words	"I think the message was confusing."
Students observing an object from many angles	"The data tell a story."
Students completing a mind map of key phrases from a speech	"His character was not convincing."
Students examining pictures of faces and naming the emotions expressed	"Here is what I think he is saying."

In the words of Mike Tyson (n.d.): "It's good to know how to read, but it's dangerous to know how to read and not how to interpret what you're reading." Readers cannot be word callers. They must read *and* interpret the meaning of what they are reading.

Examples From the CCSS: Interpret

Integration of Knowledge and Ideas: RI.4.7. Interpret information presented visually, orally, or quantitatively (e.g., in charts, graphs, diagrams, time lines, animations, or interactive elements on Web pages) and explain how the information contributes to an understanding of the text in which it appears.

Vocabulary Acquisition and Use: L.8.5,a. Demonstrate understanding of figurative language, word relationships, and nuances in word meanings.

    a. Interpret figures of speech (e.g. verbal irony, puns) in context.

TALK   Explicit Teaching Lesson

THROUGH

    In the Talk-Through, phase I, the educator teaches the thinking skill explicitly. There are several elements to aid the teacher in this phase: motivational mindset, order of operations, instructional strategy, assessment, and metacognitive reflection.

To *interpret* means to explain, to provide the meaning of something. Related terms include *construe*, *disclose*, *elucidate*, *explicate*, and *illustrate*.

Motivational Mindset

To introduce the skill of interpreting, play a sample piece of music, and ask the students to interpret the mood of the piece. They must support their interpretations with an explanation. Use three extremely different musical samples. This sets the scene to talk about interpretation and the personalization that plays a role.

Order of Operations

The process for interpreting can be summed up with the acronym XRAY:

    Examine and express the gist.

    Rank key words and phrases.

    Account for tenor and tone.

    Yield a personal opinion or interpretation.

First, an initial read is needed to examine the entirety of the piece for the gist of the idea. For example, students determine that the main idea of the following passage is that the writer must write:

"Words on paper," he told himself. "Words in the air don't matter. If I don't have words on paper I'm not a writer. I'm a talker! No words on paper, how can I improve a sentence? No words on paper, what's to work with, what's to send to the publisher, Budgeron? So simple. No mystery. Words on paper!" (Bach, 2002, pp. 16–17)

With that message in mind, students take a closer look at the words and phrasing. Words that jump out in this piece and are ranked as significant are *improve* and *publisher*, implying that the author is a professional writer. The phrase *words in the air* is an interesting way to describe talking rather than writing.

A student shares his personal interpretation or opinion of the text: "I think the author is saying that good writers write. I might also add that, in my opinion, this is a great piece to share with aspiring authors who need to spend more time writing than talking about their writing."

Instructional Strategy

The one-minute write is a great strategy to use to practice the skill of interpreting. Tell the students to get ready to write for one minute, uninterrupted, on a selected topic. They are to begin writing on the signal "Begin!" They are to stop on the signal "Hold up your pens!" Conduct the exercise as explained, timing exactly one minute.

When they have finished the task, ask them to count the number of words they wrote and put the number on their paper. Now ask them to set a goal for the next one-minute write on the same topic. They are to expand on the topic and, at the same time, try for a personal best in terms of fluency and word count. Conduct the second exercise just as you did the first. Afterward, have them count their words to determine if they met their goal and share both of their writings with a partner, who will follow the steps of XRAY.

Assessment

Have half the class watch a famous political speech with the sound off, while the other half reads the speech. Those who watch the speech base their interpretation of what was said only on the visuals; those students who read the speech base their interpretation of what was said on the words only, without nonverbal clues.

Metacognitive Reflection

Ask students to discuss with a partner or group how interpreting is different from clarifying when reading complex text.

WALK

THROUGH

Classroom Content Lesson

In the Walk-Through, phase II, teachers practice the thinking skill within content-based lessons, providing guidance to ensure the proper application of the skill. ELA Standard 10 recommends literature and instructional texts that are available for coupling with grade-level lessons.

▶ Elementary Level

Have students prepare a series of role plays about scientific phenomena by "becoming" the thing and interpreting that thing through drama. For example, students could become a magnet, a mammal, a cell dividing, a pendulum, a molecule, an atom, a plant, a bee, electricity, light, or energy.

Next, in pairs, have them read a short, selected passage in the science text and interpret the reading. Then ask them to discuss how they interpreted the thing in a dramatic way and compare that to how they interpreted the reading. Make the point that both interpretations involved making personal meaning.

▶▶ Middle Level

Require students to find an opinion page editorial about a local, state, or national concern that involves a civic issue. Have them read the article and interpret the meaning of the article. Ask them to include the source, to define significant words and phrases, and to provide their opinion of the tenor and tone of the piece. Let them share their interpretation with a partner. Sample a few with the whole class.

▶▶▶ Secondary Level

Using a statistical graph from the stock market that shows the behavior of a particular stock, have students pairs research the company, read the graph, and interpret their findings, stating their opinion of the potential of the stock. During the lesson, supply the student pairs with updated financial information so they are continually being challenged to justify their interpretation with real-time research.

DRIVE

THROUGH

CCSS Performance Task Lesson

During the Drive-Through, phase III, the thinking skill is transferred to authentic applications using CCSS performance tasks, allowing educators to make a direct connection between the selected thinking skill and the new standards. To deepen students' confidence with this skill, the teacher facilitates the student work, moving the students closer and closer to independent practice. Once the students are able to employ the skill independently, they are ready to transfer it across the curriculum. (For additional performance tasks, browse Common Core State Standards, Performance Tasks, Appendix B [NGA & CCSSO, 2010b].)

▶ Elementary Level

The following sample performance task illustrates the application of the ELA standard RI.4.7 (Reading: Informational Text, grade 4, standard 7):

> Students *interpret* the visual *chart* that accompanies Steve Otfinoski's *The Kid's Guide to Money: Earning It, Saving It, Spending It, Growing It, Sharing It* and *explain how the information* found within it *contributes to an understanding of* how to create a budget. (NGA & CCSSO, 2010b, p. 76)

▶▶ Middle Level

The following sample performance task illustrates the application of the ELA standard RI.6.8 (Reading: Informational Text, grade 6, standard 8):

> Students *trace* the line of *argument* in Winston Churchill's "Blood, Toil, Tears and Sweat" address to Parliament and *evaluate* his *specific claims* and opinions *in the text, distinguishing* which *claims* are *supported by* facts, *reasons, and evidence,* and which *are not.* (NGA & CCSSO, 2010b, p. 93)

▶▶▶ Secondary Level

The following sample performance task illustrates the application of the ELA standard RI.11–12.4 (Reading: Informational Text, grades 11–12, standard 4):

> Students *analyze how* the *key term success* is interpreted, *used, and refined over the course of* G. K. Chesterton's essay "The Fallacy of Success." (NGA & CCSSO, 2010b, p. 171)

Reflection Questions

These questions are designed to enrich your learning from doing. Such reflection enables you to deepen your understanding of the lessons you have just provided. You might also consider modifying these questions to further guide your students' reflection on this thinking skill.

1. How do you interpret student behavior based on your personal understandings of students in your discipline? What are your key triggers for forming an opinion?

2. Which habit of mind (Costa & Kallick, 2000) seems most relevant when interpreting ideas? Why?

_____ Thinking flexibly

_____ Posing questions

_____ Thinking about thinking

3. If you were to write a note to yourself about teaching your students the skill of interpreting and mail it today, what would the note say? For example, "I commit to teaching my students the explicit skill of interpreting what they hear and what they read."

4. Complete the following sentence: The most fascinating thing I learned in this chapter was . . .

3

Chapter 9: Determine

You can determine what you want. You can decide on your major objectives, targets, aims, and destination.
—W. Clement Stone

A youngster was asked to choose between two options. He could have one cent a day, doubled, for thirty days, or he could have $100,000 immediately. Even though the $100,000 seemed like a whole lot of money, he determined that it was probably a trick question, so he reluctantly chose the option of one cent a day, doubled. Once he had determined his choice, the teacher asked him to predict or estimate what the total might be. When he calculated the actual earnings of his choice, he was astonished at the total. And he was so proud that he had followed his hunch and taken the risk against his natural inclination. He had outsmarted the teacher on this one, and it felt like a victory.

The thinking skill of determining is advanced often in the CCSS. Students are asked to determine relationships, to determine key attributes, to determine the appropriate response, and to determine the central idea or theme. They are asked to determine the slope, determine the answer, and determine the mood of the story. They are also asked to determine the appropriate ratio, determine the best method for experimenting in the lab, and determine the subtleties of the relationship between the author and the point of view represented.

In essence, this skill of determining dictates the ability to see similarities and differences, to make sound judgments based on the perceived facts, and to venture a best guess with skill and grace. Make no bones about it; to determine is to risk an opinion, to see the implications of that determination, and to act on it.

To determine something in the course of reading, writing, speaking, or listening, the student must be actively involved in complex thinking. For example, the reader of a well-constructed short story must be immersed in rich details and compelled to go deeper into meaning, nuance, specifics, and word choices the author has made in order to verify or determine the author's intent. Complex text hones the skill of determining.

Table 9.1 provides examples of what this thinking skill looks and sounds like in the classroom.

Table 9.1: Determine Look-Fors and Sound Bites

Looks Like	Sounds Like
Students using a decision-tree graphic	"This makes the difference."
Students comparing and contrasting	"I think it is a competitive relationship."
Students labeling load-bearing supports in a model	"It's hard to decide."
Students identifying who is the most valuable member of a science team	"A subtle difference is . . ."
Students highlighting text	"It's difficult to see any distinction, but . . ."

To determine is a resolute act that is woven throughout everyday life, a skill used by people who are able to thoughtfully and quickly navigate the options presented in any situation.

Examples From the CCSS: Determine

Vocabulary Acquisition and Use: L.1.4. Determine or clarify the meaning of unknown and multiple-meaning words and phrases based on *grade 1 reading and content*, choosing flexibly from an array of strategies.

Key Ideas and Details: RL.7.2. Determine a theme or central idea of a text and analyze its development over the course of the text; provide an objective summary of the text.

TALK Explicit Teaching Lesson

THROUGH

In the Talk-Through, phase I, the educator teaches the thinking skill explicitly. There are several elements to aid the teacher in this phase: motivational mindset, order of operations, instructional strategy, assessment, and metacognitive reflection.

To *determine* is to settle by an authoritative or conclusive decision. Related terms include *resolve, adjust, verify, arbitrate, decide, mediate,* and *referee.*

Motivational Mindset

To set the scene for teaching the skill of determining, conduct a few right-and-wrong exercises. This is a basic determination that humans face on a fairly regular basis. Have students weigh in on one or several of the following sample dilemmas and discuss what helped them determine their opinion. Is it right or wrong:

- To double-dip with your chip
- To borrow something without permission
- To not invite a friend to an event
- To tell a white lie or omit the truth
- To refuse an invitation, or to go and not participate

Order of Operations

Determining is a sophisticated skill that involves thinking that is both analytical and evaluative. When determining something, the brain is scanning for similarities and differences; at the same time, it is evaluating the options offered. While the student is determining what the relationship is between two arguments or weighing the differences between two economic philosophies, the brain is holding the thoughts in balance. There is a systematic series of steps that occur as a determination or decision is being made. To determine similarities and differences in making a judgment or decision, key points are noted in each idea being considered, all options are put on the table, the reader or listener thinks through the various choices by analyzing and weighing the various notions, and the selected option is finally expressed. Determining could also be used when verifying point of view in a story, when deciding who is at fault in a legal case, or when resolving which compound caused a chemical reaction. This process is represented with the acronym NOTE:

Note key points.

Observe options.

Think it through and identify possibilities.

Express personal choice.

For example, as a student determines the relationship between two leaders, Lincoln and Douglas, in a historical debate, he notes the key points of each speech. Then he analyzes the opposing views for similarities and differences. The student determines the extent of the adversarial relationship between the two and draws some conclusions about their arguments in order to think through the options being offered. Finally, he clearly expresses his determination.

Instructional Strategy

Use this interactive strategy to determine relevance, relationship, nuance, central theme, and bias, or as in this case, to determine areas of concern. Post a target topic, such as college and career options. Have individual students generate comments or concerns about their own college and career options and write them on sticky notes. Then help them determine what overall themes they are facing. Have all the students look over the collection of comments generated by their fellow students, noting similarities and differences, and place the sticky notes into clusters with similar themes on a large board. Then, invite the entire group to determine all-encompassing, "generalizable" labels for the various clusters. In order to determine the labels for the various clusters that emerge, let the conversations revolve around the essence of each category. As this discussion moves forward with clarification, ideas crystallize and specific headers emerge. Finally, have the students create a verb for each label to indicate the needed action.

Assessment

Ask students to determine the value of the following skills by jotting them on sticky notes and placing them in rank order:

- Analyzing
- Evaluating
- Clarifying
- Interpreting
- Deciding
- Synthesizing

Have the students discuss their reasons for the ranking with a partner and then work to cluster the skills into at least two categories and label the clusters appropriately. Then have them add a verb to create a final label. The ranking or sequencing of the skills or ideas deepens the understanding of each as the students have to identify, evaluate, communicate, and come to consensus. Clustering the ideas around a theme and labeling that group models the act of synthesis.

Metacognitive Reflection

Have the students discuss the difficulty of determining labels for the clusters. What was hardest to do? Easiest? Why?

WALK THROUGH Classroom Content Lesson

In the Walk-Through, phase II, teachers practice the thinking skill within content-based lessons, providing guidance to ensure the proper application of the skill. ELA Standard 10 recommends literature and instructional texts that are available for coupling with grade-level lessons.

▶ Elementary Level

Have the students collect rocks from the playground or park using egg cartons for the collection boxes. Students must have a dozen rocks for the activity. Once back in the classroom, divide the students into pairs, and have them sort their twenty-four rocks into two, three, or four different categories. Then ask them to determine a name for each category. Invite each pair to share with another pair and discuss how they determined the names for their groupings and which was the hardest and the easiest to do.

▶▶ Middle Level

Assign various decades to student teams in social studies class, and ask the teams to research their designated decade and to plan and present their findings. They must determine five categories as their organizing framework and develop their presentation around those designations. Quiz the students on how they determined which categories to use to organize their presentation framework.

▶▶▶ Secondary Level

In math class, ask students to brainstorm their concerns about mathematics in a nutshell statement, using sticky notes—for example, "fear of failure." Then ask them to cluster the concerns that seem to go together and determine the labels for the clusters. Discuss their decision-making process in determining the headings.

DRIVE THROUGH CCSS Performance Task Lesson

During the Drive-Through, phase III, the thinking skill is transferred to authentic applications using CCSS performance tasks, allowing educators to make a direct connection between the selected thinking skill and the new standards. To deepen students' confidence with this skill, the teacher facilitates the student work, moving the students closer and closer to independent practice. Once the students are able to employ the skill independently, they are ready to transfer it across the curriculum. (For additional performance tasks, browse Common Core State Standards, Performance Tasks, Appendix B [NGA & CCSSO, 2010b].)

▶ Elementary Level

The following sample performance task illustrates the application of the ELA standard RI.4.2 (Reading: Informational Text, grade 4, standard 2):

> Students *determine the main idea* of Colin A. Ronan's "Telescopes" and create a *summary* by *explaining how key details support* his distinctions regarding different types of telescopes. (NGA & CCSSO, 2010b, p. 76)

▶▶ Middle Level

The following sample performance task illustrates the application of the ELA standard RI.7.4 (Reading: Informational Text, grade 7, standard 4):

> Students *determine* the *figurative and connotative meanings of words* such as *wayfaring, laconic,* and *taciturnity* as well as of phrases such as *hold his peace* in John Steinbeck's *Travels with Charley: In Search of America.* They *analyze* how Steinbeck's *specific word choices* and diction impact the *meaning and tone* of his writing and the characterization of the individuals and places he describes. (NGA & CCSSO, 2010b, p. 93)

▶▶▶ Secondary Level

The following sample performance task illustrates the application of the ELA standard RST.11–12.4 (Science & Technical Subjects, grades 11–12, standard 4):

> Students *determine the meaning of key terms* such as *hydraulic, trajectory,* and *torque* as well as other *domain-specific words and phrases* such as *actuators, antilock brakes,* and *traction control used* in Mark Fischetti's "Working Knowledge: Electronic Stability Control." (NGA & CCSSO, 2010b, p. 183)

Reflection Questions

These questions are designed to enrich your learning from doing. Such reflection enables you to deepen your understanding of the lessons you have just provided. You might also consider modifying these questions to further guide your students' reflection on this thinking skill.

1. How is the skill of determining like deciding? How is it different?

2. Discuss with your team or PLC how the skill of determining might be used effectively.

3. Complete the following sentence: When I have to come to a determination, I work best when I am . . .

Comprehensive Thinking

When applied to how people think, the adjective *comprehensive* signals the type of thinking that is both broad and deep—all encompassing. Comprehensive thinking provides us with a full grasp of the subject matter. In short, comprehensive thinking enables us to get the whole picture and comprehend it fully. For instance, if the topic of a seminar investigates the relationship of two different cultures, attendees will need to think comprehensively to understand the topic's full ramifications, infer connections that are not immediately apparent, and compare or contrast the similarities and differences in each culture. In these ways, attendees discover the full meaning of the relationships between the two cultures.

The three thinking skills in this proficiency are essential for the development of student comprehension: (1) understand, (2) infer, and (3) compare and contrast. The first, understand, is the skill that enables the student to dig deep into a significant topic or to answer a big question. The skill leads to the "I got it" element regarding the relationship between content and process.

The second skill, infer, is a sophisticated part of that basic understanding process. As students infer, or draw conclusions about what they can't see directly, they are forced to draw on secondary evidence by guessing or sniffing out the minute and sometimes invisible clues that let them read between the lines. They must rely on what they have stored in their brains from prior experiences so they can pinpoint the distinguishing factors that subtly define an idea or object and make it distinct from others.

The third skill that contributes to comprehensive thinking is comparing and contrasting. This is a dual-sided thinking skill that good readers may employ naturally but that benefits from careful nurturing. From their first years in school, students must compare and contrast colors, shapes, sizes, word shapes, and sounds; good and bad characters in a story; what is safe and what is not. In the upper grades, they compare and contrast civilizations, properties of matter, geometric shapes, story tone and tenor, and even the credibility, validity, and reliability of information they study.

Sometimes these three skills stand alone. Oftentimes, however, the full comprehension of a situation calls for their interaction. These three skills work together to provide students with not only a basic comprehension, but also a deep understanding of the texts they read and study.

Chapter 10: Understand

All truths are easy to understand once they are discovered; the point is to discover them.

—Galileo

Teacher: "What don't you understand about the word *no*?"

Student: "I don't know."

Understanding goes beyond just having a sense of what is going on; the student *knows* in a deeper way—a way that enables him or her to explain and elaborate on the idea, concept, or skill under study. To make sense, to make meaning, is implied when a student understands and comprehends.

Understanding is that foundational level of thinking that opens the doorway for more analysis, evaluation, scrutiny, and critical thinking about the topic. First, the student must grasp the meaning, getting the gist of what is there; then he or she can make determinations that are more sophisticated. With a basic understanding, students can compare and contrast, categorize, prioritize, predict, infer, and generalize.

In language arts, teachers want students to read an informational text or a fictional story with a sharp mind, identifying parts such as characters, events, symbols, and important scenes; examining characters' words and actions; finding the connections among the parts, words, and actions; and then communicating the ideas they have developed.

In math, teachers want to know how students have solved problems, why they reasoned in a certain way, and why that way ended in a logically defensible solution. Thus, *understand* implies a deeper comprehension with the ability to not only explain, but to use and apply that understanding appropriately.

The many applications of the skill *understand* all point to the same kind of thinking: making meaning, making sense of, knowing in a deep way, getting the gist of, or knowing the essence of the information. To understand is all of the above, with the implied ability to share that understanding in some way. Table 10.1 provides examples of what this thinking skill looks and sounds like in the classroom.

Table 10.1: Understand Look-Fors and Sound Bites

Looks Like	Sounds Like
Students completing a math equation on the board Students celebrating after a science experiment Students winning a debate Students completing a complex task	"I did this because . . ." "The reason for doing it this way was . . ." "The clues I used were . . ." "You will find the evidence on page . . ." "The most important ideas include . . ."

If students can't, don't, or won't read to understand, it affects everything else they do in the school arena. This leaves little doubt that understanding is most definitely a skill to teach explicitly to students as they approach narrative and informational text, as well as the speaking and listening situations that prevail in most classrooms. If students don't understand what they read or what they hear, the communication arts are not useful or productive. Understanding is the first measure of critical and creative literacy for students of all ages.

Examples From the CCSS: Understand

Presentation of Knowledge and Ideas: SL.5.4. Report on a topic or text or present an opinion, sequencing ideas logically and using appropriate facts and relevant, descriptive details to support main ideas or themes; speak clearly at an understandable pace.

Define, Evaluate, and Compare Functions: 8.F.1. Understand that a function is a rule that assigns to each input exactly one output. The graph of a function is the set of ordered pairs consisting of an input and the corresponding output.

TALK THROUGH Explicit Teaching Lesson

In the Talk-Through, phase I, the educator teaches the thinking skill explicitly. There are several elements to aid the teacher in this phase: motivational mindset, order of operations, instructional strategy, assessment, and metacognitive reflection.

To *understand* is to perceive the meaning of or grasp the idea of something. Related terms include *be aware of, be conscious of, comprehend, discern, fathom,* and *figure out.*

Motivational Mindset

To introduce the skill of understanding, ask students to pair up and tell each other a story about a time when they were expected to understand something and what happened when they did or didn't. Have them choose a topic from the following:

- To understand directions to visit a friend or a college

- To understand a joke

- To understand how to cook a hamburger

- To understand a decision that was made for them

- To understand . . . (choice option)

When finished, ask the students to identify what contributes to understanding. Make an all-class web, and add the responses.

Order of Operations

To understand an idea that is read or heard, the student needs to grasp the meaning of the main idea. Next, he or she identifies the details that support the main idea and tries to rephrase the information to make sense of it. Finally, he or she confirms the understanding by making a summary that captures the key ideas. To understand, a student must get the GIST:

Get the big idea, main idea, or theme.

Identify details to support the main idea.

Say it in your own words.

Test by creating a summary.

As students progress toward graduation from high school, the standards guide what they learn. Each year, the standards become increasingly complex. By the end of each grade, however, the grade standards return students to the same point—a deeper understanding of the content in the curriculum.

From the simple stories of kindergarten to the complex texts of the upper grades, it is essential that students sharpen the skill of understanding year by year so they can better grasp the fullest meaning of what they read. That sharpened skill is their key to success in the next year and in the world beyond their school's walls.

Instructional Strategy

There are several tools that help teachers develop their students' understanding. The National Council of Teachers of English website ReadWriteThink (www.read writethink.org) offers several interactive tools that focus on the various aspects of understanding. For example, the Writer's Cube (grades 3–12) is especially popular with students. Teachers can use the cube to teach understanding of biography, fiction, historic stories, or science time lines. By starting with student creations of their own autobiographies, teachers can use the cube to investigate what makes a good life story, one that projects meaning to the reader and reflects GIST.

Assessment

Prior to the strategy selected from ReadWriteThink, provide students with an age-appropriate rubric based on the GIST strategy (see fig. 10.1 for an example). Ask them to read a preselected piece and decide how well they understood what they read via the GIST order of operations.

Understanding	Not at All	Some	Most	Got the Picture
Get Big Idea	No vision	Blurry vision	20–20 vision	Laser-like vision
Identify Details	Empty-handed	A handful	Arms full	Wheelbarrow full
Say in Own Words	Communicated confusion	Created more questions than answers	Central point was clear	Persuaded others on the subject
Test It	Nothing connected	One detail visible	Key details exposed	All details exposed

Figure 10.1: Sample rubric for GIST.

Metacognitive Reflection

Ask students to complete the following two sentences:

1. I understand best when . . .

2. When reading a fiction story, I think I deepen my understanding when I . . .

WALK THROUGH

Classroom Content Lesson

In the Walk-Through, phase II, teachers practice the thinking skill within content-based lessons, providing guidance to ensure the proper application of the skill. ELA Standard 10 recommends literature and instructional texts that are available for coupling with grade-level lessons.

▶ Elementary Level

Provide student pairs with picture card sets that contain a square, a triangle, and a rectangle. Ask them to replicate each shape on a piece of newsprint. Tell them to identify the attributes or characteristics that are similar within each set of cards. They may circle the attribute on their drawing before you ask random pairs to explain the common elements of one figure. Check to see that all agree. Resolve disagreements before asking the pairs to draw conclusions about the similarities of each figure.

▶▶ Middle Level

Provide an age-appropriate graphic organizer for student trios. Allow each team to pick a story. In response to anchor standard 10, "read and comprehend complex literary and informational texts independently and proficiently" (NGA & CCSSO, 2010a), provide the students with time to read independently in class. Each completes the assigned graphic alone before pooling ideas with the team. As a final product, ask teams to show their understanding by creating a poster that promotes the book with reasons why all students of this age should read it.

▶▶▶ Secondary Level

Select one to two days a week or several minutes each day for silent reading. Assign a book for all in the class to read independently. After all have done the reading, have each complete a twenty-minute knowledge questionnaire about the main characters in the book. Teams can each create their own questionnaires using SurveyMonkey (www.surveymonkey.com) and exchange them with another team. Use the information you gather from the surveys as a formative assessment for the next stage of this task. Divide the class into groups of five based on the assessment results. Differentiate assignments for each team:

- Team I, lowest performers—Pick one object in the story that might be a symbol of the story's theme. Use a web to identify what characters do or say and what activities happen that support the symbol selection.

- Teams II, III, and IV, average performers—Identify one character in the story, and determine what his or her characteristics are. Compare one characteristic to a person in the group and create a Venn diagram showing similarities and differences.

- Team V, highest performers—Pick one character from the story. Identify his or her key attributes. Select a character from a current TV show as a comparison. Identify the attributes and prepare a five- to seven-page essay.

DRIVE CCSS Performance Task Lesson

THROUGH

During the Drive-Through, phase III, the thinking skill is transferred to authentic applications using CCSS performance tasks, allowing educators to make a direct connection between the selected thinking skill and the new standards. To deepen students' confidence with this skill, the teacher facilitates student work, moving the students closer and closer to independent practice. Once the students are able to employ the skill independently, they are ready to transfer it across the curriculum. (For additional performance tasks, browse Common Core State Standards, Performance Tasks, Appendix B [NGA & CCSSO, 2010b].)

▶ Elementary Level

The following sample performance task illustrates the application of the ELA standard RL.1.2 (Reading: Literature, grade 1, standard 2):

> Students *retell* Arnold Lobel's *Frog and Toad Together* while *demonstrating* their *understanding of a central message or lesson of the story* (e.g., how friends are able to solve problems together or how hard work pays off). (NGA & CCSSO, 2010b, p. 10)

▶▶ Middle Level

The following sample performance task illustrates the application of the ELA standard RST.6–8.7 (Science & Technical Subjects, grades 6–8, standard 7):

> Students *integrate* the *quantitative or technical information expressed* in the *text* of David Macaulay's *Cathedral: The Story of Its Construction* with the information conveyed by the *diagrams* and *models* Macaulay *provides*, developing a deeper understanding of Gothic architecture. (NGA & CCSSO, 2010b, p. 100)

▶▶▶ Secondary Level

The following sample performance task illustrates the application of the ELA standard RL.11–12.3 (Reading: Literature, grades 11–12, standard 3:

Students *analyze* the first impressions given of Mr. and Mrs. Bennet in the opening chapter of *Pride and Prejudice,* based on *the setting* and how the *characters are introduced.* By comparing these first impressions with their later understanding based on how *the action is ordered* and the *characters develop* over the course of the novel, students understand *the impact of* Jane Austen's *choices* in *relating elements of a story.* (NGA & CCSSO, 2010b, p. 163)

Reflection Questions

These questions are designed to enrich your learning from doing. Such reflection enables you to deepen your understanding of the lessons you have just provided. You might also consider modifying these questions to further guide your students' reflection on this thinking skill.

1. What texts do I want to select so that my students have the opportunity to increase their understanding in increasingly difficult books?

2. How can I differentiate instruction for students who are learning to read for understanding with my selection of books?

3. What other ways can I differentiate instruction about this thinking skill?

4. When teaching for understanding in my subject area, what other thinking skills do I want to stress because they are connected to understanding?

4

Chapter 11: Infer

*Scientific method, although in its more refined forms
it may seem complicated, is in essence remarkably
simple. It consists in observing such facts as will
enable the observer to discover general laws governing
facts of the kind in question. The two stages, first
of observation, and second of inference to a law,
are both essential, and each is susceptible to almost
indefinite refinement.*

— Bertrand Russell

4

"You are so wrong!" Kerry hollered at her sister. "When you don't have proof, you shouldn't infer that I did something I didn't. I didn't break your iPod."

"Says you," retorted Cali. "And besides, you don't know what you are talking about. The word you want is *imply*, not *infer*."

"What are you two arguing about now?" the girls' mother asked as she walked into the room.

"Two things: she broke my iPod, and her vocabulary stinks," snorted Cali.

"I did not, and my vocabulary is fine. She thinks she knows everything. I do know that a speaker or writer implies, and a listener or reader infers."

"You're right on that," Mrs. Anderson said. "So, Cali, what's your evidence that it was Kerry who broke your iPod?"

Sherlock Holmes is the master inference maker. He is the ultimate detective, finding clues most others miss, putting them together in ways no one else would think of, and discovering conclusions that always solve the deepest mystery. The scientist follows the same thinking regimen. Starting with a theory, based first on facts, the scientist gathers more and more evidence, until he or she reaches a verifiable conclusion, or inference, with a sufficient amount of reliable data.

Authors, especially poets, turn the table on students. What they imply challenges for their readers to infer. In one sense, readers have to assume the Sherlock Holmes' role and go looking for clues about what they are reading. When they find the clues, they deepen their enjoyment of and involvement with the fictional word by making judgments about the characters and events.

Nonfiction writers are less circumspect. Rather than ask the reader to infer meaning from clues, the nonfiction writer presents the facts and guides the reader to a preordained conclusion. It is up to the reader to judge whether the literal data provided are necessary and sufficient for the stated conclusion.

Infer is often referred to as "reading between the lines." It searches for the meaning that is sometimes hidden below the surface of the text. Inferred meaning is hinted at, implicit, not the predominant melody but background notes that thread through the piece.

Table 11.1 provides examples of what inferring looks and sounds like in the classroom.

Table 11.1: Infer Look-Fors and Sound Bites

Looks Like	Sounds Like
Students examining a fossil to determine its age	"My best guess is . . ."
Students improvising with another actor	"Reading between the lines, I . . ."
Students discussing the meaning of a poem	"I concluded . . ."
Students reading body language	"The clues tell me that . . ."

Making sound and reliable inferences is one of the most difficult challenges young people face in and out of school. In school, students are required to infer almost daily in literature, science, social science, and mathematics. Fiction writers often plant hidden clues to paint the distinctions that separate one character from another, often revealing key attributes. Lady MacBeth's bloody hands declare her role in the murder, but they also give clues about the depth of her guilt. In science, social science, and math, facts and numbers are presented that students must add up or put together to draw logical conclusions; they have to make inferences from stated and observed information.

Outside of school, drawing inferences is no less important. From the earliest crib days, young children learn to read the faces of parents and siblings. As they grow older, they learn to study the words and actions of their peers. With these clues, they learn to form friendships or go a different way. Reading between the lines also helps people determine whether they should trust what they read, hear, or see.

Essentially, inferring is the skill of gathering data, reading situations or people, and making sense of what is seen, felt, and heard. It is a necessary skill for all learners. With a sharp ability to draw valid and logical conclusions from available evidence, students are ready to figure out the complexities of the world around them.

Examples From the CCSS: Infer

Making Inferences and Justifying Conclusions: S-IC.1. Understand statistics as a process for making inferences about population parameters based on a random sample from that population.

Vocabulary Acquisition and Use: L.7.4d. Verify the preliminary determination of the meaning of a word or phrase (e.g., by checking the inferred meaning in context or in a dictionary).

TALK THROUGH Explicit Teaching Lesson

In the Talk-Through, phase I, the educator teaches the thinking skill explicitly. There are several elements to aid the teacher in this phase: motivational mindset, order of operations, instructional strategy, assessment, and metacognitive reflection.

To *infer* is to come to a logical explanation or conclusion based on observations and/or facts. Related terms include *conjecture*, *deduce*, *derive*, *glean*, and *reason*.

Order of Operations

Inferring is looking beyond the obvious to understand the spin or slant put on the information. Students must investigate the facts, note the details, find a common thread, and explain the connections made that lead to a conclusion. This process is represented with the acronym INFER:

Investigate the facts.

Note all details.

Find the common thread.

Explain the connections.

Reach your conclusion.

In Shakespeare's Sonnet 18, he compares his lover to a summer's day, providing the reader with a list of comparisons that justify this love. It is the reader's job not only to enjoy the words, the metaphors, the rhymes, and the clever use of iambic pentameter, but also to glean how all the comparisons are tied together as an impassioned plea for her love. Once that thread is apparent, it becomes easy for the reader to deduce how all the parts of the poem fit together to show a deep expression of the author for his beloved.

In the Shakespeare example, the reader must investigate the facts for meaning, note all the details of language that lend credence to the words, find the common thread of passion and love, explain the connection between passion and love, and reach the conclusion that this love will defy even death.

Instructional Strategy

Select an appropriate grade-level poem from the recommended list in CCSS, Standard 10. Display the poem for the whole class to see, and read the poem. After the reading, ask the students to (a) tell you what the poem says, (b) explain what is implied by the author, and (c) determine what they can infer. Highlight the words *say*, *imply*, and *infer* in your questions before making a list of answers from their responses for all to see. Discuss the importance of each word, especially in language arts. Have the students apply the INFER process to see what makes sense, even if it is not explicitly stated.

Assessment

Invite students to share their self-assessments of making inferences. Ask for explanations about the cues and clues they use to make inferences when they read and to share what they find difficult when trying to draw an inference. Have them use INFER as a guide to help them make this assessment specific.

Metacognitive Reflection

Have students complete the following sentence: When I read between the lines, I find it most helpful to . . .

WALK THROUGH

Classroom Content Lesson

In the Walk-Through, phase II, teachers practice the thinking skill within content-based lessons, providing guidance to ensure the proper application of the skill. ELA Standard 10 recommends literature and instructional texts that are available for coupling with grade-level lessons.

▶ Elementary Level

In the classroom, on the playground, and in other appropriate locations in the school, post clues about characters in a book read by all the students. Send the students on a clue search. When the clues come back, invite students to try to match their clues as in a jigsaw puzzle. Provide poster board for each character so that students can attach the clues. After all clues are attached, randomly assign each student to a poster board. Ask the students to explain what the clues say about their character and to connect their ideas to what they had read in the story, making inferences that make sense from the information. Hang an INFER poster to which they can refer on a regular basis.

▶▶ Middle Level

After your students have read an age-appropriate teacher-selected novel, divide them into teams of three, and ask them to create an attribute web on a large sheet of newsprint. The central shape of the web is a symbol that the team believes represents the character. The rays shooting out from the symbol are the words and phrases in the text that support the use of this symbol with this character. Teams post the webs for a carousel discussion, during which they cite specific textual evidence to support their support conclusions.

▶▶▶ Secondary Level

Ask teams of students to select an age group in the community (no duplicates). As a class, prepare a health survey that covers all the groups and determine a number of persons to survey. Have the teams select a sampling method they have studied. After gathering the data, each team uses the data to estimate the mean, which is charted on poster board. The class asks appropriate questions, and the team defends its sampling method. When each question session is done, the focus team draws a conclusion or inference about its sampling method and returns to an assessment via INFER.

DRIVE CCSS Performance Task Lesson

THROUGH During the Drive-Through, phase III, the thinking skill is transferred to authentic applications using CCSS performance tasks, allowing educators to make a direct connection between the selected thinking skill and the new standards. To deepen students' confidence with this skill, the teacher facilitates the student work, moving the students closer and closer to independent practice. Once the students are able to employ the skill independently, they are ready to transfer it across the curriculum. (For additional performance tasks, browse Common Core State Standards, Performance Tasks, Appendix B [NGA & CCSSO, 2010b].)

▶ Elementary Level

The following sample performance task is an example of the application of the ELA standard RL.4.1 (Reading: Literature, grade 4, standard 1):

> Students *explain* the selfish behavior by Mary and make *inferences* regarding the impact of the cholera outbreak in Frances Hodgson Burnett's *The Secret Garden* by *explicitly referring to details and examples from the text.* (NGA & CCSSO, 2010b, p. 70)

▶▶ Middle Level

The following sample performance task illustrates the application of the ELA standard RL.6.1 (Reading: Literature, grade 6, standard 1):

> Students *cite explicit textual evidence* as well as draw *inferences* about the drake and the duck from Katherine Paterson's *The Tale of the Mandarin Ducks to support* their *analysis* of the perils of vanity. (NGA & CCSSO, 2010b, p. 89)

▶▶▶ Secondary Level

The following sample performance task illustrates the application of the ELA standard RL.11–12.1 (Reading: Literature, grades 11–12, standard 1):

> Students *cite strong and thorough textual evidence* from John Keats's "Ode on a Grecian Urn" to *support* their *analysis* of what the poem says explicitly about the urn as well as what can be *inferred* about the urn from *evidence* in the poem. Based on their close reading, students *draw inferences from the text* regarding what meanings the figures decorating the urn convey as well as noting *where the* poem *leaves matters about the urn and its decoration uncertain.* (NGA & CCSSO, 2010b, p. 163)

Reflection Questions

These questions are designed to enrich your learning from doing. Such reflection enables you to deepen your understanding of the lessons you have just provided. You might also consider modifying these questions to further guide your students' reflection on this thinking skill.

1. What rubrics can you build to guide your observations of students developing their inference skills?

2. What can you say or do to help parents appreciate the value of the thinking skill of making inferences?

3. Complete the following sentence: It is important for students to develop
   inference skills in my class because . . .

4

Chapter 12:
Compare and Contrast

Under the surface of contradiction lies similarity.
—Asif Jordan

―――――――――――

"My favorite sport? I'm not sure," Thomas said.

"Thomas likes any sport. As long as he can move." His mom chuckled.

"He plays hockey more than any other—all year round," his sister Anna said.

"Well, when you compare how much time I spend, I guess hockey is my favorite."

In their first months, babies recognize an increasing number of faces. Very early on, they distinguish the features of their parents from those of others who pick them up. When young children begin to read, they discriminate letters and sounds, recognize complex emotions that signal different reactions, and determine detailed similarities and differences in pictures. Progressing through the school years, children sharpen their abilities to compare and contrast all that they capture with their senses. Whether in math, science, fine arts, literature, or social sciences, their minds group likenesses and separate differences in what they see, hear, and read.

Most children come to find it easy to pick the precise words for grouping objects that are alike. They learn to sort by color, shape, odor, size, number, and texture. They can create attribute webs or lists focused on a single quality in multiple examples: "Which objects in this room are blue? Round? Long? Short?" Even when contrasting two similar objects, young students often find it simple to list the characteristics that make the difference and note that "this is a pencil and that is a pen because . . ."

In the middle grades, as students move to more abstract thinking, some begin to experience difficulty with comparisons. For instance, when asked to complete a Venn diagram showing the similarities and differences between Asian and African elephants, many find it easy to note the physical traits they see or hear. But beyond the obvious, some students struggle with finding anything to say about the more subtle likenesses and differences.

There are those students who have not yet developed the abstract thinking processes needed to perceive anything beyond the concrete similarities (such as size, shape, and color). They are trapped in the literal. For instance, when asked to compare two characters in a story, students who have not developed their inferring skills may struggle to name any characteristics that relate to how the character might be feeling or how the character thinks and plans.

The ELA standards not only call for students to employ these twin skills of comparing and contrasting, but these standards raise the ante to ensure that students will show the progress made in being able to apply these skills in increasingly complex learning tasks.

Table 12.1 provides examples of what the compare-and-contrast thinking skill looks and sounds like in the classroom.

Table 12.1: Compare and Contrast Look-Fors and Sound Bites

Looks Like	Sounds Like
Students completing a Venn diagram	"I see how they are alike."
Students sorting science specimens	"The opposing point is . . ."
Students labeling for classification	"I see how they are different."
Students debating an issue	"This is not exactly the same because . . ."
	"A different point of view is . . ."

The compare-and-contrast thinking skill is a basic cognitive skill. It is learned in the earliest years of life, determines early success in school, and leads the way to development of the mega skill of understanding. It doesn't stand alone; it relies on other thinking skills, such as inferring, analyzing, synthesizing, and evaluating. In their more subtle forms, compare and contrast suggest distinguishing or differentiating.

The compare-and-contrast skill has applications in every phase of students' lives. When they go to the grocery store, they do comparison shopping. When they walk home, they differentiate their house from the neighbors' homes. They compare and contrast clothes, test scores, smartphones, grades, and TV shows they like.

In school, students can't advance without developing the skill of comparing and contrasting. In fact, Robert Marzano et al. (2001) declare the skill of finding similarities and differences to be the a top-ten skill in terms of high-yield strategies in student achievement.

Examples From the CCSS: Compare and Contrast

Craft and Structure: RL.2.6. Acknowledge differences in the points of view of characters, including by speaking in a different voice for each character when reading dialogue aloud.

Integration of Knowledge and Ideas: RST.6–8.9. Compare and contrast the information gained from experiments, simulations, video, or multimedia sources with that gained from reading a text on the same topic.

TALK Explicit Teaching Lesson

THROUGH

In the Talk-Through, phase I, the educator teaches the thinking skill explicitly. There are several elements to aid the teacher in this phase: motivational mindset, order of operations, instructional strategy, assessment, and metacognitive reflection.

To *compare* is to show likeness or similarities, to note sameness. Related terms include *equate, liken, match, correspond,* and *parallel.* To *contrast* is to show the differences between two or more things. Related terms include *differ, deviate, vary,* and *separate.*

Motivational Mindset

To pique students' interest in the skill of compare and contrast, ask them to work with a partner and determine how they are alike and different. After the pairs find their similarities and differences, ask them to talk about which was easier to do, compare or contrast.

Order of Operations

When comparing and contrasting ideas, objects, people, and events, there are a number of critical thinking steps, represented by the acronym ALIKE:

Account for literal similarities and differences.

Look again; don't miss the obvious.

Investigate the hidden details of likeness and difference.

Know the categories.

Express in alternating or dual descriptions.

For example, students complete a very brief comparison of two cars, a Ford and a Toyota, using the ALIKE process. They first account for the obvious similarities and differences: the Ford is bigger and the color is brighter than the Toyota; the Ford's is more expensive. Then they look again for more data: the Toyota is a hatchback, and the Ford has a normal trunk space. Investigating further, they find that the Ford is made in America by an American company, and the Toyota is made in America by a Japanese company. The Toyota is in a category of "all options included," while the Ford is in the category of "all options extra." The students express their summary of the two: the Ford is more expensive with fewer amenities, while the Toyota is more appealing to the eye and has lots of desirable options. While this is a simplistic example of the ALIKE process, it demonstrates the thinking that is involved in comparing and contrasting.

Instructional Strategy

Divide the students into cooperative groups of three, and assign them two wild animals. Allow students to conduct research on the animals, both print and online. Then ask the teams to create a Venn diagram comparing and contrasting the two animals and prepare to present their work to the whole class.

Assessment

Prior to the teams' work on their Venn diagrams, present an assessment rubric that will identify how many differences and similarities they should find and what evidence they should pick to illustrate both.

After student teams complete their Venn diagrams, invite one team to post its diagram for all to see. After noting what the first team presented and its match to the rubric, invite at least two other teams to present and contrast their diagrams so the class can build a final diagram that represents the most complete set of comparisons and contrasts.

Metacognitive Reflection

Ask the students to answer the following questions:

- When you were making a comparison of the two animals, what clues were most important?

- When you were contrasting the Venn diagrams from the different teams, what clues did you look for?

- How did the Venn diagrams help make more complete and precise comparisons or contrasts?

WALK

THROUGH

Classroom Content Lesson

In the Walk-Through, phase II, teachers practice the thinking skill within content-based lessons, providing guidance to ensure the proper application of the skill. ELA Standard 10 recommends literature and instructional texts that are available for coupling with grade-level lessons.

▶ Elementary Level

Assign the students to groups of three. Provide a sufficient number of stories so each group has its own book with at least three characters. Invite the students to take turns reading the story aloud to each other before each selects a character to act out in a different voice. After they demonstrate their story to their group, ask the students to explain why they selected the different voices and prepare a presentation that compares and contrasts the voices.

▶▶ Middle Level

Give students twelve separate math problems: four of them use only digits, four of them are story problems, and four of them use geometric shapes. Have the students solve all twelve, and then in pairs, compare and contrast attributes of the three different formulas. Ask them to answer the questions: Which was the easiest to solve, and why? Which was the hardest to solve, and why? Which formula is more practical for real-world applications, and why? To facilitate the students' thinking, walk among the teams to listen and ensure they are answering the questions asked.

▶▶▶ Secondary Level

Divide the class into teams, and have each team choose a novel from a list of important books that have movie versions. Tell the team to read the novel first, with each person on the team concentrating on one character. Afterward, students review their character on the movie by focusing on what the character says and does and what others say about the character. Have them use a Venn diagram to collect the information. When they are finished, invite each to make a poster board contrasting the presentation of the character in each medium.

DRIVE   CCSS Performance Task Lesson

THROUGH

During the Drive-Through, phase III, the thinking skill is transferred to authentic applications using CCSS performance tasks, allowing educators to make a direct connection between the selected thinking skill and the new standards. To deepen students' confidence with this skill, the teacher facilitates the student work, moving the students closer and closer to independent practice. Once the students are able to employ the skill independently, they are ready to transfer it across the curriculum. (For additional performance tasks, browse Common Core State Standards, Performance Tasks, Appendix B [NGA & CCSSO, 2010b].)

▶ Elementary Level

The following sample performance task illustrates the application of the ELA standard RL.5.9 (Reading: Literature, grade 5, standard 9):

> Students *compare and contrast* coming-of-age *stories* by Christopher Paul Curtis (*Bud, Not Buddy*) and Louise Erdrich (*The Birchbark House*) by identifying *similar themes* and examining the stories' *approach* to the topic of growing up. (NGA & CCSSO, 2010b, p. 70)

▶▶ Middle Level

The following sample performance task illustrates the application of the ELA standard RL.7.9 (Reading: Literature, grade 7, standard 9):

> Students *compare and contrast* Laurence Yep's *fictional portrayal of* Chinese immigrants in turn-of-the-twentieth-century San Francisco in *Dragonwings to historical accounts of the same period* (using materials detailing the 1906 San Francisco earthquake) in order to glean a deeper *understanding* of *how authors use or alter historical sources* to create a sense of *time* and *place* as well as make fictional *characters* lifelike and real. (NGA & CCSSO, 2010b, p. 89)

▶▶▶ Secondary Level

The following sample performance task illustrates the application of the ELA standard RL.11–12.9 (Reading: Literature, grades 11–12, standard 9):

> Students compare and contrast how the protagonists of Herman Melville's *Billy Budd* and Nathaniel Hawthorne's *Scarlet Letter* maintain their integrity when confronting authority, and they relate their *analysis* of that *theme* to other portrayals in *nineteenth- and early-twentieth-century foundational works of American literature* they have read. (NGA & CCSSO, 2010b, p. 163)

Reflection Questions

These questions are designed to enrich your learning from doing. Such reflection enables you to deepen your understanding of the lessons you have just provided. You might also consider modifying these questions to further guide your students' reflection on this thinking skill.

1. How could you reinforce the ALIKE process with your students?

2. Analyze the grade-level curriculum, and brainstorm ways to intensify the explicit instruction of compare and contrast.

3. What additional strategies can you use to develop your students' skills at understanding similarities and differences?

4

Collaborative Thinking

While collaboration is an acknowledged skill of the global community, it is also an essential skill of the school community. In fact, according to numerous studies (Johnson & Johnson, 1975, 2010; Joyce & Weil, 1995; Kagan, 1994; Marzano et al., 2001; Sharan, 1990; Slavin, 1996), it is the number-one proficiency in terms of student achievement. It is a proficiency with its own benefits—collaboration, problem solving, and leadership—but it also facilitates the implementation of other high-yield classroom strategies, like comparing and contrasting.

Collaboration has been examined for essential component parts that contribute to a successful structure: teamwork, communication, leadership, and conflict resolution. More specifically, teamwork refers to invested members working toward a common goal, communication refers to a skillfulness that fosters a back-and-forth sharing of ideas, leadership skills showcase the strengths and talents of each member, and conflict resolution skills allow teams to move forward despite differences.

Embedded in this atmosphere of collaboration are three specific skills that affect the results of the group effort: (1) explain, (2) develop, and (3) decide. To *explain* implies a two-way communication between the explainer and the receiver of the explanation and confirmation of message received. To *develop* implies that the explanations result in collaborative, ongoing progress. Finally, to *decide* implies that a sound outcome results from fruitful collaborations.

Chapter 13: Explain

If you can't explain it simply, you don't understand
it well enough.

                                        —Albert Einstein

Lamenting the lack of skill and understanding students have about algebra, middle school teacher Mr. Pedley said, "The question asked for students to show their work. This is what I got from Peter."

Name: *Peter*

Question #6

Expand: $(a + b) - y$

$$= (a+b) - y$$
$$= (a + b) - y$$
$$= (a + b) - y$$
$$= (a + b) - y$$

Ms. Meyers enjoyed the unexpected response of the student and got a good laugh, but sensing the frustration of her colleague, she tried to respond appropriately: "Thanks for sharing your story. That picture tells it all. You must be a bit exasperated, but you have to admit, he tried."

"Yeah, he tried, but my worry is, it's either a hilarious joke on me or a very sad note on the state of affairs in my algebra class."

"Well, either way, as the English teacher, I love it. You know what they say, 'Stories stick and stay, but facts fade away.' It makes the mark in my book for a great explanation on his part. He showed the skill as he understood it."

In developing the cooperative skills and collaborative spirit of teamwork, the ability to listen attentively is important. To listen with attention means that the conversation sometimes involves paraphrasing, affirming, clarifying, and testing options. When an explanation is given in a collaborative process, there are explicit, attentive listening techniques that should accompany the explanation.

A closer look shows that paraphrasing is the key to understanding. When students can repeat or paraphrase in their own words, they anchor the learning. Another listening technique is affirming what someone is saying, signaling that the listener is with the speaker. That occasional nod or intermittent "uh-huh" lets the speaker know that the listener is there and hearing what the speaker saying. Clarifying questions also acts as a signal that the communication is being received. The questions serve to push the explanation to more detail and elaboration. Finally, the concept of testing options is a tool for attentive listening. Testing options sounds like: "What if . . . ?" or "Yes, but . . ." or "What about . . . ?" While explaining is an essential skill for collaboration, attentive listening is a natural partner in the discussion.

Both "how" and "why" explanations support deep thinking about complex texts and help students in their collaborative tasks. Table 13.1 provides examples of what explaining looks and sounds like in the classroom.

Table 13.1: Explain Look-Fors and Sound Bites

Looks Like	Sounds Like
Students talking using hand gestures	"I'm wondering why . . ."
Students talking to a partner	"Let me show you."
Students using a story as an example	"First, . . . second, . . . and third, . . ."
Students pointing to a time line and talking	"That explains it for me."
Students using a manipulative to show . . .	"Your explanation is not clear to me."

The skill of explaining is basic to most real-world communications and is essential to productive and meaningful collaborations. It is used in giving directions: "Let me explain how to get there"; in describing processes or products: "Can you explain how this works?"; and in clarifying communications: "I want to explain in terms that are understandable to all."

Examples From the CCSS: Explain

Key Ideas and Details: RL.4.1. Refer to details and examples in a text when explaining what the text says explicitly and when drawing inferences from the text.

Algebra: A-SSE.3. Choose and produce an equivalent form of an expression to reveal and explain properties of the quantity represented by the expression.

TALK

THROUGH

Explicit Teaching Lesson

In the Talk-Through, phase I, the educator teaches the thinking skill explicitly. There are several elements to aid the teacher in this phase: motivational mindset, order of operations, instructional strategy, assessment, and metacognitive reflection.

To *explain* is to make something plain or clear, understandable or intelligible. Related terms include *articulate, tell, comment on, illuminate, illustrate, interpret, justify, make more explicit,* and *paraphrase.* In practice, when students are required to show their work and state the steps they used in solving a problem, they are actually being asked to explain their thinking in an explicit way and to track it on paper.

Motivational Mindset

To begin the lesson on the skill *explaining*, provide each student with a cartoon. In pairs, students explain to their partner what is happening in the cartoon. The partner can either add to what has been said or ask a question. Then, they change roles. Make the point that explaining is a basic communication skill that needs to be honed for use in many different circumstances.

Order of Operations

Under examination, the explicit teaching of the skill of explaining seems to sift into a simple process. A statement of the big idea begins the explanation, which is usually supported with a telling detail or two. The explanation proceeds with any other details necessary for clarity. Finally, the explainer listens for any questions and responds appropriately. The process is represented by the acronym TELL:

5

Tell the big idea.

Express supporting statements.

Look for more details.

Listen for questions and respond.

For example, after class on Friday, a student explains to a buddy how to get to the campground. He says, "The quickest, most direct way to get there is to go by the corner gas station and take the first right." He continues with a supporting statement: "You'll notice a little sign that says 'Caroga Lake' just as you turn onto that road." He pauses as he tries to think of any other details. He then says, "I can't remember the name, for sure, but I think it might say, 'Route 10.'" His buddy asks, "How far is it from there? And, is it on the right or left?" The student provides his buddy with this additional information.

Instructional Strategy

Have your students practice the TELL order of operations by creating sandwich words. Choose a topic, such as friendship. With the class, brainstorm a list of words that are relevant to the topic. Have student pairs create a new word by combining two words from the list to create a big idea. The new word needs an explanation, so have the pairs provide a pseudo-dictionary definition. Invite students to listen for imagined questions and add details to create a full description, complete with a sample sentence.

For example, the topic is friendship. Generated words include *buddy, trust, loyal, longtime, honest, reliable, fun, comfortable, time, patient, play, interests, dependable, partner, understanding, Facebook, long lasting, laughter, support, listener,* and *kind.*

Sandwich word #1: Plartner (combining *play* and *partner*)

> **Definition:** Plartner (noun)—a good friend who will always be your partner during playtime

> **Sample sentence:** When it is time for recess, Bobby and I go together because we are plartners.

Sandwich word #2: Buddstanding (combining *buddy* and *understanding*)

> **Definition:** Buddstanding (noun)—the ability of good friends to always comprehend what the other is saying or feeling

> **Sample sentence:** What Betty said may not have made sense to you, but I understood her perfectly because of our buddstanding.

Assessment

Ask the students to explain to a partner why it is important to know the history of words and their meanings.

Metacognitive Reflection

Have students write their responses to these questions: Was this open-ended assignment easier or harder than an assignment from the book? Why or why not?

WALK Classroom Content Lesson

THROUGH

In the Walk-Through, phase II, teachers practice the thinking skill within content-based lessons, providing guidance to ensure the proper application of the skill. ELA Standard 10 recommends literature and instructional texts that are available for coupling with grade-level lessons.

▶ Elementary Level

Have students work in pairs to read a picture book. One student reads a passage, and then the other explains how the picture in the book supports what the author has written. They take turns reading and explaining until the end of the book. Then invite the pairs to think of a story they both know and explain to each other what pictures would be appropriate to include in the story.

▶▶ Middle Level

Have the class assemble ten to fifteen vocabulary words from their reading list. Ask the students to choose a partner and create a sandwich word and a dictionary definition for the word, complete with an explanation of the meaning and a sample sentence incorporating the word. Then have them share the new word with other teams. Debrief the class by naming three elements that are needed for a clear explanation.

▶▶▶ Secondary Level

Divide the class into pairs. Have the students scan the text for significant words and compile a list of ten to twenty. Ask them to cluster the words, create two sandwich words, and write an explanation of what the words mean, following the TELL process. Once they finish, have them share their words and explanations with other teams.

Debrief the class with what makes a good, great, and grand explanation. What are the ingredients that matter? Then, apply the skill of explaining to an illuminating episode in the text.

DRIVE CCSS Performance Task Lesson

THROUGH

During the Drive-Through, phase III, the thinking skill is transferred to authentic applications using CCSS performance tasks, allowing educators to make a direct connection between the selected thinking skill and the new standards. To deepen students' confidence with this skill, the teacher facilitates the student work, moving the students closer and closer to independent practice. Once the students are able to employ the skill independently, they are ready to transfer it across the curriculum. (For additional performance tasks, browse Common Core State Standards, Performance Tasks, Appendix B [NGA & CCSSO, 2010b].)

▶ Elementary Level

The following sample performance task illustrates the application of the ELA standard RL.3.7 (Reading: Literature, grade 3, standard 7):

> Students *explain* how Mark Teague's *illustrations* contribute to what is conveyed in Cynthia Rylant's *Poppleton in Winter* to *create the mood and emphasize aspects of characters and setting* in the story. (NGA & CCSSO, 2010b, p. 53)

▶▶ Middle Level

The following sample performance task illustrates the application of the ELA standard RH.6–8.5 (History/Social Studies, grades 6–8, standard 5):

> Students *describe how* Russell Freedman in his book *Freedom Walkers: The Story of the Montgomery Bus Boycott* integrates and *presents information* both *sequentially* and *causally* to explain how the civil rights movement began. (NGA & CCSSO, 2010b, p. 100)

▶▶▶ Secondary Level

The following sample performance task illustrates the application of the ELA standard RST.11–12.1 (Science & Technical Subjects, grades 11–12, standard 1):

> Students *analyze* the concept of mass based on their close reading of Gordon Kane's "The Mysteries of Mass" and *cite specific textual evidence* from the *text* to answer the question of why elementary particles have mass at all. Students explain *important distinctions the author makes* regarding the Higgs field and the Higgs boson and their relationship to the concept of mass. (NGA & CCSSO, 2010b, p. 100)

Reflection Questions

These questions are designed to enrich your learning from doing. Such reflection enables you to deepen your understanding of the lessons you have just provided. You might also consider modifying these questions to further guide your students' reflection on this thinking skill.

1. An effective way to teach or explain concepts is by storytelling. How can teachers use storytelling in their explanations embedded in their lessons? Share an example of how you already teach using storytelling.

2. Have you ever considered that a disciplinary measure may be an opportunity to teach students the skill of explaining? How might you turn a disciplinary measure into such a teachable moment?

3. Considering that an explanation given by someone not familiar with the topic can be time consuming, how can the skill of explaining fit into a crowded classroom curriculum?

5

Chapter 14: Develop

*An acquaintance that begins with a compliment is
sure to develop into a real friendship.*

—Oscar Wilde

A mom called to her son, who was in his bedroom, "Why do you read about those dinosaurs all the time? You need to get out and do things with your friends."

The son called back, "I don't do it all the time, just when I have some time."

"But why is it so important to you that you can't take a minute to socialize and enjoy the day? You have your head buried in a book or are online every waking hour of the weekend."

"Mom, you know what I told you before. To become an expert at something takes ten thousand hours of study and practice. If I want to develop into a prize-winning champion, I'll have to practice intensely for ten years. Well, I want to be an archeologist, and to be the best one, I have to put in the time."

"What are you talking about? You're eleven."

"Yeah, but that means if I keep working hard, I'll be twenty-one when I am expert enough."

The more the individuals in a group work together, the more their collaborative expertise develops and grows. There is a developmental path that often occurs as collaborations are advancing through various stages. The four stages of developing skillful collaborations include: (1) forming, (2) norming, (3) storming, and (4) performing (Bellanca & Fogarty, 2003; Tuchman, 1965). In fact, it is much like the path that professional learning communities often follow. The first stage is formally putting the group together or forming the collaborative. Then, once the team begins to collaborate, the norming process evolves and norms develop as the accepted behaviors of the group. As the collaborations develop into nitty-gritty tasks, with robust and rigorous conversations, a third stage of the collaborative process emerges, storming. This is when the team members are struggling to reach a consensus and finding ways to agree to disagree and move on. Ironically, storming is a sign of healthy collaborations, because it demonstrates the development from placating people to offering different perspectives and different views. The final stage in the process of developing a sound team is the performing stage. Performing as a tightly knit team of individuals requires commitment and dedication to the higher cause.

Table 14.1 provides examples of what this thinking skill looks and sounds like in the collaborative classroom.

Table 14.1: Develop Look-Fors and Sound Bites

Looks Like	Sounds Like
Students with their heads together in conversation A student leaning in toward a partner Students gathering at a table Students listening attentively A student indicating a point on a chart	"What about this idea?" "I like what I am hearing." "I agree." "You're exactly right." "Yes, but . . ."

The story at the beginning of the chapter explores the concept of developing as an expert, while in the introductory text we discussed developing as part of collaboration. In either case, the concept of developing requires mindfulness. Developing an idea is much different than having an idea, and this real-world skill of how to develop one's thoughts is sorely needed for student work in all disciplines. Students must learn how to take an initial idea and develop it in full detail and to take the idea to completion. Voicing an opinion on the op-ed page of the local newspaper or on a favorite blog is very different from tweeting a 140-character thought about it.

TALK THROUGH   Explicit Teaching Lesson

In the Talk-Through, phase I, the educator teaches the thinking skill explicitly. There are several elements to aid the teacher in this phase: motivational mindset, order of operations, instructional strategy, assessment, and metacognitive reflection.

To *develop* is to bring out the capabilities or possibilities of something or to bring to a more advanced or effective state. Related terms include *disclose, elaborate, evolve, exhibit, form, materialize, untwist, unwind,* and *achieve.*

Examples From the CCSS: Develop

Text Types and Purposes: W.7.3. Write narratives to develop real or imagined experiences or events using effective technique, relevant descriptive details, and well-structured event sequences.

Production and Distribution of Writing: W.9–10.5. Develop and strengthen writing as needed by planning, revising, editing, rewriting, or trying a new approach, focusing on addressing what is most significant for a specific purpose and audience.

Motivational Mindset

Have the students imagine that a textbook has been invented that has all of the answers to every question any student will ever need to know to complete his or her education and graduate. Their quick assignment is to develop a title and a slogan for the book.

Order of Operations

Developing ideas or strategies can be an independent endeavor, but in this discussion, it is placed in the context of collaborative thinking and teamwork. The acronym MAKE illustrates how collaborative teams develop ideas beyond the talking stage and into realized goals:

Meet to discuss the issue.

Ask questions.

Kick ideas around.

Express the goal and plan.

To develop ideas, team members must first find a time and location in which to meet and discuss the issue. Once the issue is on the table, team members more often than not will start to ask relevant and pertinent questions to develop the idea further. That usually leads to a more heated interchange in which ideas are kicked around to develop a fuller picture, which, sooner or later, must develop into a well-articulated plan that is expressed fully, if meaningful results are to occur.

Instructional Strategy

Problem scenarios are often used to express a challenge or problem that needs attention. Using "students trying to find balance between schoolwork and extracurricular activities" as the target topic, lead a whole-group discussion about this issue. Ask clarifying questions and help students see the idea from many perspectives. Then divide the students into groups of five, and have them create a problem scenario around one of the ideas they discussed as a class. They have to title the scenario, write a short description, and then develop three possible solutions.

For example, a scenario may be titled "Join Every Club." The description may be: "You are concerned that your GPA and entrance exams will not be enough to get you into your dream school so to beef up your résumé, you decide to join some clubs. Soon you find that all of your time is spent preparing to attend or attending meetings. Your schoolwork is beginning to suffer. What will you do?"

Explain that they must use the MAKE strategy when developing both the scenario and the solutions.

Assessment

Develop a student-designed handbook for incoming high school freshmen that will help them with the pressure of college preparation.

Metacognitive Reflection

Give students the beginning of a story line and ask them to develop a surprise or unexpected ending to the situation presented. Use picture book stories, historical scenarios, or current events that are playing out in the news. The idea is to have them develop an ending that is plausible but not necessarily probable.

WALK THROUGH   Classroom Content Lesson

In the Walk-Through, phase II, teachers practice the thinking skill within content-based lessons, providing guidance to ensure the proper application of the skill. ELA Standard 10 recommends literature and instructional texts that are available for coupling with grade-level lessons.

▶ Elementary Level

Teach the students how to create problem scenarios, and then assign them to create their own problem scenarios based on a unit of study in science or social studies. Assign stakeholder roles: "You are . . . What will you do?" Have students discuss the situations and try to come up with alternative solutions.

For example, in a science class, student teams are asked to create possible problem scenarios that an explorer may encounter when traveling to the Arctic. They then exchange scenarios and provide three possible solutions.

▶▶ Middle Level

Demonstrate a problem scenario, and model how to develop three different solutions to problem solve the scenario. Then have students work in small groups of three to four and brainstorm problems and challenges the community or city faces (such as graffiti, crime, parks for kids, public transportation for elderly, dogs off leashes, and so on). Ask them to develop an open-ended scenario for one of the challenges that begins with "You are . . ." and ends with "What will you do?" Have them pass their scenario to another group, which will generate three solutions for the scenario.

▶▶▶ Secondary Level

Ask pairs of students to develop scenarios about careers or college using stakeholder roles and open-ended questions: "You are a . . . What will you do?" In the next period, have them exchange scenarios with another pair and develop responses to the scenario, which will be included in a presentation.

DRIVE CCSS Performance Task Lesson

THROUGH

During the Drive-Through, phase III, the thinking skill is transferred to authentic applications using CCSS performance tasks, allowing educators to make a direct connection between the selected thinking skill and the new standards. To deepen students' confidence with this skill, the teacher facilitates the student work, moving the students closer and closer to independent practice. Once the students are able to employ the skill independently, they are ready to transfer it across the curriculum. (For additional performance tasks, browse Common Core State Standards, Performance Tasks, Appendix B [NGA & CCSSO, 2010b].)

▶ Elementary Level

The following sample performance task illustrates the application of the ELA standard RL.1.1 (Reading: Literature, grade 1, standard 1):

> Students (*with prompting and support from the teacher*) when listening to Laura Ingalls Wilder's *Little House in the Big Woods* *ask questions about* the events that occur (such as the encounter with the bear) and *answer* by offering *key details* drawn from the *text*. (NGA & CCSSO, 2010b, p. 28)

▶▶ Middle Level

The following sample performance task illustrates the application of the ELA standard RL.6.6 (Reading: Literature, grade 6, standard 6):

> Students *explain how* Sandra Cisneros's choice of words *develops the point of view of the* young *speaker in* her story "Eleven." (NGA & CCSSO, 2010b, p. 89)

▶▶▶ Secondary Level

The following sample performance task illustrates the application of the ELA standard RL.11–12.3 (Reading: Literature, grades 11–12, standard 3):

> Students *analyze* the first impressions given of Mr. and Mrs. Bennet in the opening chapter of *Pride and Prejudice* based on *the setting* and how the *characters are introduced.* By comparing these first impressions with their later understanding based on how *the action is ordered* and the *characters develop* over the course of the novel, students understand *the impact of* Jane Austen's *choices* in *relating elements of a story.* (NGA & CCSSO, 2010b, p. 163)

Reflection Questions

These questions are designed to enrich your learning from doing. Such reflection enables you to deepen your understanding of the lessons you have just provided. You might also consider modifying these questions to further guide your students' reflection on this thinking skill.

1. Read this quote: "You must take action now that will move you toward your goals. Develop a sense of urgency in your life" (Browne, 1965). How might your PLC or team develop a sense of urgency in the school about 21st century skills? Why would you do that?

2. Using a standards-based traditional lesson, write a problem scenario for students. How might you invite them into the investigation and turn the lesson into an inquiry lesson?

3. Complete the following sentence: I would like to develop . . .

Chapter 15: Decide

Nothing is more difficult, and therefore more
precious, than to be able to decide.

—Napoleon Bonaparte

Two high school students were moving a piano for the music director. They were asked to put it somewhere out of the way until after the parent conferences. As they moved down the hallway, headed for the stairwell, they were noticeably laboring and struggling with the weight and size of the piano. One of the boys said, "I don't think we are ever going to get this thing up to the fourth floor."

His partner said, "Up? I thought we were taking it down."

Moral of the story: decide where you are going, or you won't know when you get there.

To decide—to make a decision and settle on a final outcome—is an act of evaluation, prioritization, and commitment. Decision making is no easy task as one must weigh the pros and cons, or the strengths and weaknesses, of the various options, but to do this in a collaborative environment, in which multiple opinions abound, is even more difficult. Deciding as a team involves a complex matrix of effective communication, clarity of thought, effectiveness of arguments, and willingness to compromise, and the decision requires commitment if it is to succeed fully.

Table 15.1 (page 132) provides examples of what this thinking skill looks and sounds like in the collaborative classroom.

Table 15.1: Decide Look-Fors and Sound Bites

Looks Like	Sounds Like
Students creating charts of pros and cons	"How many agree?"
Students filling out a T-chart for strengths and weaknesses	"Let's look at the options."
	"What are the pros? Cons?"
Students participating in team meetings	"My decision is based on . . ."
Students with their heads together	"I prefer this one because . . ."
Students voting	

Deciding is a necessary skill if students are to become productive problem solvers and creative innovators, both in and out of school. There is no college, career, or life situation in which decision making does not play a role.

Examples From the CCSS: Decide

Comprehension and Collaboration: SL.11–12.2. Integrate multiple sources of information presented in diverse formats and media (e.g., visually, quantitatively, orally) in order to make informed decisions and solve problems, evaluating the credibility and accuracy of each source and noting any discrepancies among the data.

Making Inferences and Justifying Conclusions: S-IC.5. Use data from a randomized experiment to compare two treatments; use simulations to decide if differences between parameters are significant.

TALK Explicit Teaching Lesson

THROUGH

In the Talk-Through, phase I, the educator teaches the thinking skill explicitly. There are several elements to aid the teacher in this phase: motivational mindset, order of operations, instructional strategy, assessment, and metacognitive reflection.

To *decide* is to solve or conclude a question, controversy, or struggle by giving victory to one side. Related terms include *resolve*, *award*, *choose*, *conclude*, *decree*, and *establish*.

Motivational Mindset

To introduce the skill of *decide*, ask students to pair up and talk about their decision-making processes. They should share the answers to the following questions:

- How do you balance work and play?

- What is your favorite thing to do when you have free time?
- What is your decision-making process?

This activity works best if each partner talks about the first question before moving on to the second question and so on, so there is more back-and-forth conversation about making decisions.

Order of Operations

Decision making is a process that embraces a series of steps to arrive at that final decision. It is often a time-consuming task that requires robust interactions to understand the entire situation. The KNOW acronym delineates this process:

Know all the options.

Note the pluses and minuses, pros and cons.

Outline probable, possible, and preferable solutions.

Welcome a decision, and celebrate.

Everyone, including students, makes decisions automatically, as part of their everyday lives. Being aware of their decision-making process and being able to reflect on and improve their process is another issue entirely.

Instructional Strategy

Create a differentiated lesson on the Civil War that requires students to make decisions about how they will represent what they have learned. The assignment is to write an essay about the Civil War using one of four focuses: (1) the people, (2) the causes, (3) the outcomes, and (4) the battles. Students decide which will be their focus using the process of KNOW.

First, they have to know all their options, the people, the causes, the outcomes, and the battles. Then they note the pluses and minuses of each possible option by listing the pros and cons. Next they outline probable obstacles to overcome, possible resources they can depend on, and preferable solutions. Finally they welcome a decision and begin their essay with the focus they have decided on.

The decision-making process continues at this point. For example, if they choose to write an essay with a focus on the people, they will have to decide whether to write about a group of people, a specific family, or an individual. Decisions have to be made regarding whether these people represented the North or the South, if they were historically significant, or if they were simply a representative of a type of people that contributed to the history of the Civil War.

Each step of the way, require the students to use the KNOW order of operations to work through their decisions and to make clear their thinking processes in addition to the final essay on the Civil War.

Assessment

Have students apply the KNOW decision process in another assignment in another subject area, giving details of how it might have improved the final assignment.

Metacognitive Reflection

Have students respond to the question: do you agree or disagree with the statement "A good decision-making process always results in a good decision"? Why or why not?

WALK THROUGH   Classroom Content Lesson

In the Walk-Through, phase II, teachers practice the thinking skill within content-based lessons, providing guidance to ensure the proper application of the skill. ELA Standard 10 recommends literature and instructional texts that are available for coupling with grade-level lessons.

▶ Elementary Level

Ask students, in a whole-group discussion, to decide the top five most popular books for their grade level by using the KNOW process. All students may nominate books for consideration with a justification statement, which is then followed by a group discussion. Then all students decide by voting with secret ballot. The celebration involves all five books featured with a poster of their covers on the bulletin board for Parent Night.

▶▶ Middle Level

Have students research and decide using the KNOW process which five U.S. government documents are most important for teenagers to be familiar with. Students must nominate and justify their document choice with three valid reasons. Discussions and question-and-answer sessions are followed by secret ballot voting, rating each candidate document on a scale of one to ten. Totals decide the winning five. Celebrations for the decision involve the reading of the first paragraphs of the five winning documents on the school's PA system.

▶▶▶ Secondary Level

Have the students research and decide using the KNOW process which are the five most important scientific discoveries to impact the world as we know it. They must present each candidate discovery in a team presentation that includes vital information. Students will decide on the top five through discussions of the pros and cons of each and then by a final and secret ballot voting. The winning five will be shared in an artistic display in the entrance hall showcase.

DRIVE CCSS Performance Task Lesson

THROUGH During the Drive-Through, phase III, the thinking skill is transferred to authentic applications using CCSS performance tasks, allowing educators to make a direct connection between the selected thinking skill and the new standards. To deepen students' confidence with this skill, the teacher facilitates the student work, moving the students closer and closer to independent practice. Once the students are able to employ the skill independently, they are ready to transfer it across the curriculum. In each example, the skill *decide* is implied, not exactly stated. (For additional performance tasks, browse Common Core State Standards, Performance Tasks, Appendix B [NGA & CCSSO, 2010b].)

▶ Elementary Level

The following sample performance task illustrates the application of the ELA standard RI.K.4 (Reading: Informational Text, grade K, standard 4):

> Students *ask and answer questions about* animals (e.g., hyena, alligator, platypus, scorpion) they encounter in Steve Jenkins and Robin Page's *What Do You Do With a Tail Like This?* (NGA & CCSSO, 2010b, p. 36)

▶▶ Middle Level

The following sample performance task illustrates the application of the ELA standard RL.6.1 (Reading: Literature, grade 6, standard 1):

> Students *cite explicit textual evidence* as well as draw *inferences* about the drake and the duck from K. Paterson's *The Tale of the Mandarin Ducks to support* their *analysis* of the perils of vanity. (NGA & CCSSO, 2010b, p. 89)

▶▶▶ Secondary Level

The following sample performance task illustrates the application of the ELA standard RI.11–12.6 (Reading: Informational Text, grades 11–12, standard 6):

> Students determine Richard Hofstadter's *purpose and point of view* in his "Abraham Lincoln and the Self-Made Myth,"

analyzing how both Hofstadter's *style* and *content contribute* to the *eloquent* and *powerful* contrast he draws between the younger, ambitious Lincoln and the sober, more reflective man of the presidential years. (NGA & CCSSO, 2010b, p. 171)

Reflection Questions

These questions are designed to enrich your learning from doing. Such reflection enables you to deepen your understanding of the lessons you have just provided. You might also consider modifying these questions to further guide your students' reflection on this thinking skill.

1. List ten on-your-feet decisions you made today.

2. Use the KNOW process on a personal decision, such as a big-item purchase, vacation plans, or career choice. Then have your students do the same kind of activity with their parents.

3. Rank your personal experience with decision making and complete this sentence: Decision making is _____ for me because . . .

   ▶ A breeze

   ▶ Sorta easy

   ▶ Deliberative

   ▶ Kinda hard

   ▶ Agonizing

Communicative Thinking

What do researcher Michelle Dawson, inventor Temple Grandin, composer Hikari Ōe, wildlife illustrator Dylan Pierce, and Australian author Donna Williams have in common? All of these brilliant minds are challenged with autism. In their younger years, these famous individuals struggled to communicate by spoken word with most people who met them. The fault was not in the listeners, nor in the speakers. Each one of these people with high-functioning minds found it difficult to speak with precise language just what was on his or her mind.

Although these are special cases, there are many students who are inhibited by one challenge or another when explaining what they want others to understand. Communication doesn't work well. Sometimes the break is with the spoken word. Other times, it is with the written word.

Teachers may often assume that this inability to communicate is due to the person's mental ability. However, this is seldom the case. Some students have difficulty gathering the information they need to understand an idea. Blind and dyslexic students face this challenge. Others lack skill in processing information. Others still struggle with communicating. Teachers can help these students strengthen their communicative skills, especially in classrooms that intentionally adopt project-based learning and active inquiry instruction. Both models provide teachers with multiple opportunities to integrate written and spoken communication for daily instruction and practice.

The skills of *reasoning, connecting*, and *representing* are critical to the expression of meaning. These communicative skills appear in all subject areas as essential means for presenting information to another's ears or eyes. The ability to reason is to be able to make logical sense of ideas as the first step toward communicating ideas. In like manner, connecting is a highly relevant skill that synthesizes facts, data, and other input into meaningful patterns. These chunks of information help students consolidate ideas and create and present relevant findings to others. Finally, the third skill, representing, allows the presenter to transform words into images or vice versa so listeners and readers can picture the concept or fact. All three are directly connected to making sense of information and sharing that interpretation with others.

Chapter 16: Reason

*People are generally better persuaded by the reasons
which they have themselves discovered than by those
which have come in to the mind of others.*

—Blaise Pascal

After Julie dropped the bus fare in the box, she took the third aisle seat. To
her astonishment, the other passenger in the seat addressed her: "Well, Mrs.
Peterson. Where are you going today?"

Julie asked the lady if they had met before.

"Oh, no. I have never laid eyes on you before you got on the bus."

"Then how did you know my name?" Julie asked.

"Oh, that is easy," the lady responded. "The tag on your satchel gives your name,
and the ring on your finger says you are married. It's simple logic, and I'm good
at reasoning."

The act of reasoning has rules. A must follow B with a sufficient line of evidence.
All the facts selected must contribute to the argument. No facts may be extraneous
or unconnected. Each one says something, and when they are connected, we reach
a conclusion.

"What's your reason?" or "Why do you think that?" is the most important question
teachers can ask after students have presented an answer. In providing their reason,
students must offer an explanation of a situation or circumstance that made certain
results seem possible or appropriate. Sometimes the reason is tight and clear, as in the
case of cause and effect: the weak center support collapsed, causing the bridge to fall.

In other instances, the connection evidence is weak or muddled. When some of the facts prove to be unconnected to the effect or result or when there are not enough valid facts, a reason is weak.

Reasoning is a two-step act. First, the student uses logic to arrive at a conclusion. Second, he or she communicates that reasoning to others to convince them of the conclusion. Table 16.1 provides examples of what this thinking skill looks and sounds like in the classroom.

Table 16.1: Reason Look-Fors and Sound Bites

Looks Like	Sounds Like
A student proving a math equation	"What's your reasoning?"
Students engaged in a mock trial	"Are these facts connected to this case?"
A student describing how he solved a puzzle	"What facts are we missing?"
A student team discussing which project to choose	"What is your evidence?"
A student offering a conclusion for a failed experiment	"What is your justification?"

Reasoning is what humans do. We take clues and draw conclusions. The challenges to reason well are found in every life situation and career field. After employing reason to make logical sense of a situation or challenge, the person often is called upon to explain the line of reasoning taken.

Doctors reason as they diagnose mysterious illnesses: "What do the facts tell me? Can I read these facts and find a reasonable answer that will restore my patient's health?" They sit with the patient, explain the diagnosis, and communicate the reasons for a proposed line of treatment.

Police reason as they look at the clues at a crime scene: "What details do I see? Can I read these clues and find the guilty party?" Later in court, the officer must communicate to the judge the logical thinking that put the clues together to prove a person's guilt.

Brokers reason as they follow the financial trends: "What is happening that will give me proof that I should buy or sell?" After the trade, the brokers go to their clients to explain their rationale. Communication is the key to the transaction.

Plumbers reason as they search for the source of a leak: "How do I follow this trail systematically to the most likely source?" Once it is found, they communicate what work is required and the reasons for doing that work on a specific schedule.

Computer programmers reason as they follow a logical code to write a new software solution: "What are the rules that I must follow to do this?" After writing the new code, they communicate it to their client.

Teenagers reason as they argue for new rights: "If I am old enough to drive a car, then I must be old enough to stay out an extra hour." Again, communication is key to the interaction.

In these many different situations, the individuals call on the power of reasoning to reach a logical conclusion and then persuade others of the conclusion's rationality.

Examples From the CCSS: Reason

Text Types and Purposes: W.3.1. Write opinion pieces on topics or texts, supporting a point of view with reasons.

   a. Introduce the topic or text they are writing about, state an opinion, and create an organizational structure that lists reasons.

   b. Provide reasons that support the opinion.

   c. Use linking words and phrases (e.g., *because, therefore, since, for example*) to connect opinion and reasons.

Presentation of Knowledge and Ideas: SL.11–12.5. Make strategic use of digital media (e.g., textual, graphical, audio, visual, and interactive elements) in presentations to enhance understanding of findings, reasoning, and evidence and to add interest.

TALK THROUGH   Explicit Teaching Lesson

In the Talk-Through, phase I, the educator teaches the thinking skill explicitly. There are several elements to aid the teacher in this phase: motivational mindset, order of operations, instructional strategy, assessment, and metacognitive reflection.

To *reason* is to come to a conclusion by thinking logically and to communicate a position based on logic. Related words include *argue, deduce, derive, advocate, surmise, rationalize, contend,* and *assert.*

Motivational Mindset

A quick and motivating way to introduce the thinking skill of reasoning is with the game Give Me a Reason. Brief interactions highlight reasoning skills as part of everyday conversations and negotiations. AB partners role-play, A as the adult (parent, teacher, or coach) and B as the student. Use the following as examples:

Partner B asks, "May I stay at my friend's house tonight?"
Partner A replies, "Give me a reason that makes sense."

Partner B says, "I want to go to college out of state."
Partner A replies, "Give me a reason that makes sense."

Partner B asks, "Is it OK if I miss practice tomorrow?"
Partner A replies, "Give me a reason that makes sense."

Partner B says, "I want an after-school job."
Partner A replies, "Give me a reason that makes sense."

Discuss as a class some reasons that students give in these dialogues and judge which truly make sense.

Order of Operations

As with all higher-order thinking processes, reasoning requires a series of steps. The first step is to look at the facts and determine what's important and what's not. Then it's helpful to offer connecting details that provide support to the initial facts gleaned about the situation. Next, gather obvious and not-so-obvious explanations that seem logical. Identify the most likely reason, the one that makes the most sense with the evidence at hand. Finally, conclude with what seems to be the best reason for the outcome, and communicate that conclusion in some way. Use the acronym LOGIC to remember this process:

Look at all the facts.

Offer connecting details.

Gather explanations.

Identify the most sensible reason.

Conclude and communicate.

For example, two students are arguing about what constitutes a lie. One contends that a lie is explicitly speaking a mistruth, while the other insists that not telling something you know is the same as lying. To add a little more to their case, they offer details to support the argument. The first one claims that lying is an action, while the other says that a lie can be implied. They then gather explanations from each side. The first says, "If I say I like your outfit and I really don't like it, I am telling an outright lie." The second student retorts, "I agree, but if you didn't like it and you didn't say anything at all because you didn't want to hurt my feelings, you'd be lying by withholding the truth." Now they identify the best explanation: "If we agree that lying is intentional and deceitful, both of our examples fit the category." Finally, they can conclude and communicate this logic: it is a lie to intentionally deceive, whether the lie is explicit or implicit.

Instructional Strategy

A fun activity with which to engage students in the skill of reasoning is a comic strip activity. Pass out a six-frame comic strip template. This reproducible is found in appendix A on page 192.

Read the first half of a selected story. Have students fill in the first three scenes on their comic strips based on what was read and then trade with a partner. Then ask them to fill in the last three scenes, predicting, based on the facts, what will happen in the second half of the story. All should prepare reasons for their selections based on text evidence before the teacher reads the last half of the story to see what happens.

Assessment

Ask students to create a rubric based on their discussions of what they now think are good reasons for an action. Brainstorm a list of ideas and then vote to get the top four. Save this rubric for the metacognitive reflection.

Metacognitive Reflection

Ask students to think about the following questions and then provide specific examples with their answers:

- How reasonable am I when I am arguing my point of view on something?
- Do I use facts or emotion to make my case?
- How do I measure up to the criteria on our class rubric when I am trying to prove a point?

WALK **Classroom Content Lesson**

THROUGH

In the Walk-Through, phase II, teachers practice the thinking skill within content-based lessons, providing guidance to ensure the proper application of the skill. ELA Standard 10 recommends literature and instructional texts that are available for coupling with grade-level lessons.

▶ Elementary Level

Identify a controversial issue in your classroom, such as cell phone use. Using a pro/con chart, engage in a whole-group discussion. When all points seem to have been made, have the students determine whether they are for or against the issue and give reasons for their conclusions.

▶▶ Middle Level

Ask students to agree or disagree with the concept of gender-specific classes in their middle school. Have them list the pros and cons and provide logical arguments for their conclusions.

▶▶▶ Secondary Level

Some educators take the position that students should not receive zeros for missing work, teachers should not average grades for a term grade, and there shouldn't be any killer assignments that are worth a huge percent of the final grade. Instead, teachers should assign a term grade for the student's final standing at the end of the course. Discuss these ideas with the class, and ask students to weigh in with logical reasons for their stances. Post the reasons for all to see, and if time allows, ask the class to rate the strength of the reasons.

DRIVE   CCSS Performance Task Lesson

THROUGH

During the Drive-Through, phase III, the thinking skill is transferred to authentic applications using CCSS performance tasks, allowing educators to make a direct connection between the selected thinking skill and the new standards. To deepen students' confidence with this skill, the teacher facilitates the student work, moving the students closer and closer to independent practice. Once the students are able to employ the skill independently, they are ready to transfer it across the curriculum. (For additional performance tasks, browse Common Core State Standards, Performance Tasks, Appendix B [NGA & CCSSO, 2010b].)

▶ Elementary Level

The following sample performance task illustrates the application of the ELA standard RI.4.8 (Reading: Informational Text, grade 4, standard 8):

> Students *explain how* Melvin Berger *uses reasons and evidence* in his book *Discovering Mars: The Amazing Story of the Red Planet* to *support particular points* regarding the topology of the planet. (NGA & CCSSO, 2010b, p. 76)

▶▶ Middle Level

The following sample performance task illustrates the application of the ELA standard RI.6.8 (Reading: Informational Text, grade 6, standard 8):

Students *trace* the line of *argument* in Winston Churchill's "Blood, Toil, Tears and Sweat" address to Parliament and *evaluate* his *specific claims* and opinions *in the text, distinguishing* which *claims* are *supported by* facts, *reasons, and evidence,* and which *are not.* (NGA & CCSSO, 2010b, p. 93)

▶▶▶ Secondary Level

The following sample performance task illustrates the application of the ELA standard RI.11–12.8 (Reading: Informational Text, grades 11–12, standard 8):

Students *delineate* and *evaluate* the *argument* that Thomas Paine makes in *Common Sense*. They *assess the reasoning* present in his analysis, including the *premises and purposes* of his essay. (NGA & CCSSO, 2010b, p. 171)

Reflection Questions

These questions are designed to enrich your learning from doing. Such reflection enables you to deepen your understanding of the lessons you have just provided. You might also consider modifying these questions to further guide your students' reflection on this thinking skill.

1. When is student reasoning most evident in your classroom?

2. Descartes said, "I think, therefore I am." How does his statement apply to your teaching of the skill of reasoning?

3. As you look back over your facilitation of this thinking skill, what have you learned about the teaching of reasoning and how can you improve?

6

Chapter 17: Connect

Believing that the dots will connect down the road
will give you the confidence to follow your heart, even
when it leads you off the well-worn path.

—Bill Gates

"You're making no sense. What do you mean I stood you up?" Tom asked.

"You were supposed to meet me at the music counter. We were going to look at the new white iPhone," Leo responded.

"Couldn't be. My scheduler says I was supposed to be at kung fu practice. That's my guide for the day. It's how I make my schedule, my connections. You know, like connecting the dots for the sequence of the day."

"Well, somehow, you missed a dot, and you missed our connection!"

In essence, connecting is a skill in combining, synthesizing, and interpreting how various elements go together. Connecting is discerning patterns, seeing likenesses and differences, and finding the perfect slot for the new idea.

Written and spoken words not only say what they mean, but they also suggest other meanings. In each context, the thinking person has to combine all the clues in order to make sense of the situation. In narrative text, an inflection, a nod, a smile, or a frown connects to other clues to change the meaning of a single word. In informational text, connections between people, places, and things are relevant to the communicated meaning. How are the people connected in this historical event? What does the place at which people shop have to do with their food choices? How do the cause-and-effect connections play out in this science experiment?

The mind must make connections and associations to consolidate and chunk information for storage and subsequent retrieval. Thus, making critical connections in reading, writing, speaking, and listening is an active part of the communications process.

The skill of making connections can be taught explicitly, practiced endlessly, and honed in all grade levels and across all content areas. It is important to recognize that students make sense of new information by making connections, by connecting the dots, perceiving relationships, and noticing how ideas are associated. Making connections is a high-level cognitive process that is very different from memorizing facts. The brain is a meaning-making machine, searching through patterns to find a fit for the new information. Time is well spent when teachers stir up prior knowledge to help the brain make these connections.

Through experience, students learn to view information with questioning eyes and to ask, "How does all this connect?" rather than impulsively jumping to a conclusion. As students consider all the facts, including their own prior experiences, they learn to select those details that seem to have the closest and strongest connections. When they have as complete a picture as possible, they communicate to others the reasons for each connection. Table 17.1 provides examples of what connecting looks and sounds like in the classroom.

Table 17.1: Connect Look-Fors and Sound Bites

Looks Like	Sounds Like
Students completing graphic organizers	"The picture is clear if these are linked."
Students linking two ideas from two different chapters	"I see the connection."
Student teams color-coding a textbook	"I think that this goes with this . . ."
Students tracing ideas on a wall map	"They go in this order."
Students labeling lines on an organizational chart	"I see how A and B match."

In connecting ideas, students learn to ask questions such as, "How are causes related to effects?" and "How are events connected in time, place, and type?" In answering such questions, students go far beyond memorized facts. While making connections makes learning in the daily curriculum easier and more successful, students may also use this skill outside of school, noting how incidents in the neighborhood or political events are connected, for instance.

Examples From the CCSS: Connect

Vocabulary Acquisition and Use: L.3.5b. Identify real-life connections between words and their use (e.g., describe people who are *friendly* or *helpful*).

Text Types and Purposes: WHST.9–10.2,a. Write informative/explanatory texts, including the narration of historical events, scientific procedures/experiments, or technical processes.

  a. Introduce a topic and organize ideas, concepts, and information to make important connections and distinctions; include formatting (e.g., headings), graphics (e.g., figures, tables), and multimedia when useful to aiding comprehension.

TALK THROUGH Explicit Teaching Lesson

In the Talk-Through, phase I, the educator teaches the thinking skill explicitly. There are several elements to aid the teacher in this phase: motivational mindset, order of operations, instructional strategy, assessment, and metacognitive reflection.

To *connect* is to join, link, or associate, to bring together as a whole. Related terms include *attach*, *bridge*, *conjoin*, *correlate*, *hook up*, *interface*, and *couple*.

Motivational Mindset

To introduce students to the thinking skill *connect*, play a game called Bricks and Mortar. The bricks represent big ideas, and the mortar is the glue that holds the ideas together.

Using subject-specific topics, name a topic, and have students supply comprehensive sentences related to the topic, noting context connections. For example, the topic, or *brick*, is "legislative." The *mortar* that the first student mentions is, "It's one of the three branches of government." The second student, who must make another connection, says, "It makes the laws in the two houses of Congress." This contextual gluing continues for several rounds, to build meaningful connections to the topic.

Order of Operations

Making connections involves several mental operations. Students must judge the information that is important, observe obvious connections that the mind races to, identify the pattern that fits, and name the connection that makes sense. The acronym for this process is JOIN:

Judge the new information for telling facts.

Observe obvious connections.

Identify patterns, and find a fit.

Name the connection that makes sense.

For example, a high school class reads the following poem:

> *The well-made book,*
> *climbs from the shelf,*
> *it says*
> *I'm here*
> *because somebody gave a damn*
> *and worked with someone else*
> *who gave a damn,*
> *and together they made me possible*
> *and says all this quietly,*
> *albeit firmly.*
> *It has texture and depth*
> *so that it almost breathes.*
> *It is filled with the dignity*
> *of common labor,*
> *and somewhat mirrors human fallibility:*
> *there is no perfect book.*
>
> —Anonymous

The students first look for facts in the poem: "It's about the collaborative labor that goes into writing a book." Then, to make sense of this, the students make obvious connections. The mind may turn to a familiar book and think about how it appealed to them from the library or bookstore shelf. Now, they identify a pattern it fits with: "This is a narrative poem that tells a story." Finally, as they grasp the meaning, they name the connection that makes sense to them: "I have never really thought about how much work goes into a book and that there are others involved to make the whole thing happen. It's like the work that goes into my writing and the feedback I get from peer editing and from the teacher."

Instructional Strategy

The KWL chart, attributed to Donna Ogle (1986), is an effective tool to access prior knowledge for making explicit connections. It is meant to act as a graphic organizer for whole-group or small-group interactions.

Choose a topic from your current unit of study. Provide each table team with a KWL chart; a blank KWL chart can be found in appendix A on page 193. Have them complete the chart by listing five to seven things they know about the topic in the first column, What I Know. This is where they will connect to their knowledge and understanding from prior experiences and background knowledge they all have. Then ask them to list five to seven things that they want to learn about the topic in the second column, What I Want to Know. Here they will make connections to what they know with questions they have and curiosities that have been aroused by stirring up their prior knowledge.

Once they have completed the two columns, have them share and compare with another group. If circumstances allow, revisit the KWL chart at the end of the class and complete the third column, What I Learned, as a whole group.

Assessment

Have the students complete the following as journal entries:

- The KWL can help me . . .
- If I were to make a checklist about connecting prior knowledge, I would include . . .
- The most important thing I learned from this lesson about making connections is . . .

Metacognitive Reflection

Ask students to consider the following question: when you are puzzled about something you don't understand, what do you do to help you make the appropriate connections?

Classroom Content Lesson

In the Walk-Through, phase II, teachers practice the thinking skill within content-based lessons, providing guidance to ensure the proper application of the skill. ELA Standard 10 recommends literature and instructional texts that are available for coupling with grade-level lessons.

▶ Elementary Level

Take the students on a walk in the neighborhood around the school. Point out important buildings (stores, churches, homes, and such). Back in the classroom, give students a template sketch of the blocks walked. Ask them to sketch in the important buildings they saw. Invite them to share with a partner one specific building in the neighborhood and their personal connection to it. After partner talk, sample several student answers and debrief the class on the value of making personal connections to the experience.

▶▶ Middle Level

Plan a research project that aligns with a grade-appropriate ELA standard and allows for students to present to the class. For instance, assign groups of three to investigate the life of a historic character. Teach them to do library research or online research about the character. After the research, have each student make a personal connection to the character under study and write a paragraph about the connection, which he or she will present to the class. Discuss how making connections—text to another text, text to a world situation, or text to self—are reading strategies that help students connect to the text with real understanding (Anderson, Hiebert, Scott, & Wilkinson, 1984).

▶▶▶ Secondary Level

Ask trios to select a poem. (See a list of age-appropriate text suggestions from CCSS Standard 10). Invite the students to identify an important metaphor or analogy in the poem; interpret the selection with evidence from the poem and the author's life, beliefs, and times; and make and explain a visual display (poster, website, multimedia) of how that metaphor connects to a timely issue today. Have a class display with presentations.

DRIVE CCSS Performance Task Lesson

THROUGH
During the Drive-Through, phase III, the thinking skill is transferred to authentic applications using CCSS performance tasks, allowing educators to make a direct connection between the selected thinking skill and the new standards. To deepen students' confidence with this skill, the teacher facilitates the student work, moving the students closer and closer to independent practice. Once the students are able to employ the skill independently, they are ready to transfer it across the curriculum. (For additional performance tasks, browse Common Core State Standards, Performance Tasks, Appendix B [NGA & CCSSO, 2010b].)

▶ Elementary Level

The following sample performance task illustrates the application of the ELA standard RI.K.3 (Reading: Informational Text, grade K, standard 3):

> Students (*with prompting and support from the teacher*) *describe the connection between* drag and flying in Fran Hodgkins and

True Kelley's *How People Learned to Fly* by performing the "arm spinning" experiment described in the text. (NGA & CCSSO, 2010b, p. 28)

▶▶ Middle Level

The following sample performance task illustrates the application of the ELA standard RL.8.2 (Reading: Literature, grade 8, standard 2):

Students *summarize the development* of the morality of Tom Sawyer in Mark Twain's novel of the same name and analyze its connection to themes of accountability and authenticity by noting how it is conveyed *through characters, setting, and plot.* (NGA & CCSSO, 2010b, p. 89)

▶▶▶ Secondary Level

The following sample performance task illustrates the application of the ELA standard RI.9–10.3 (Reading: Informational Text, grades 9–10, standard 3):

Students *analyze how* Abraham Lincoln in his "Second Inaugural Address" *unfolds* his examination of the *ideas* that led to the Civil War, paying particular attention to *the order in which the points are made, how* Lincoln *introduces and develops* his points, *and the connections that are drawn between them.* (NGA & CCSSO, 2010b, p. 129)

Reflection Questions

These questions are designed to enrich your learning from doing. Such reflection enables you to deepen your understanding of the lessons you have just provided. You might also consider modifying these questions to further guide your students' reflection on this thinking skill.

1. How do you go about using a standard to guide the design of an activity or lesson that connects to students in a relevant way?

2. How might you work with a partner or two to design a project that will challenge students to focus on making connections between two different subject areas? Included should be the requirement that a presentation of their project must provide an explanation of the way their ideas connect the two subjects.

3. Complete the following sentence: I connect best with my students when I . . .

Chapter 18: Represent

In order to represent life on the stage, we must rub elbows with life, live ourselves.

—Marie Dressler

"Look, Mother! A rainbow. Isn't it beautiful?"

"Yes," said the mother. "And do you know what it represents?"

The boy shook his head.

"It means that you are going to have nothing but good luck for the next year."

"Oh wow!" exclaimed the boy. "For real?"

"Well, yes and no," his mother said. "The rainbow is real. It is made by the sun's reflection off water droplets in the sky. But it is also just a fairytale. Some people believe that the rainbow represents good luck. It's a symbol for them. It gives them hope and joy."

The skill *represent* requires one to show, illustrate, or provide a rendition of the information. Drawings, illustrations, web pages, dramas, role plays, PowerPoint presentations, iMovies, collages, dioramas, inventions, podcasts, posters, symbolic figures and codes, and cartoons—all can be acceptable representations that demonstrate evidence of learning. When students are given options for providing evidence of learning, they own the learning.

It is important to note that even though this skill of representing works through various modalities, *represent* is not explicitly stated as a high-frequency ELA word. However, there are many standards in which the skills of producing and presenting, illustrating, and showing results are prevalent. Words that might allude to this same thinking skill of representing information within the ELA standards include *demonstrate, produce, depict, illustrate, show, prove, reproduce*, and *draw*.

Represent appears often in the Mathematics standards. In this context, it refers to showing how a math operation can be demonstrated or illustrated in different forms to clarify and exhibit understanding.

Students have many means of representing their understanding at their fingertips. The more skillful they become in representing their ideas, the more skillful their communications skills become. It is most definitely a skill that needs attention.

Table 18.1 provides examples of what this thinking skill looks and sounds like in the classroom.

Table 18.1: Represent Look-Fors and Sound Bites

Looks Like	Sounds Like
Students creating a storyboard of the events in a novel Students acting out the process of metamorphosis Students building a scale model of the solar system	"I forgot the symbol for greater than." "I need the symbolic language for pi." "This geometric shape changes to . . ." "How do you show area and perimeter?" "This collage tells them what they need to know."

Representing information is a critically important skill for students. One reason involves *receptive language skills*, and the other targets *expressive language skills*. Receptive language skills, the taking in of information either through reading, sensing, or listening, involve the knowledge and understanding of representational language—symbols and signs that are embedded in the text. Symbolic language is extremely abstract, and yet it is extremely critical to understanding as one reads or views incoming information that is in code. When receiving these codes, perhaps a series of dots and dashes or a photo of a red rose, the receiving person has to call on layers of prior experience and mix and match them until arriving at a determination of the hidden or suggested meaning.

Using expressive language skills to represent one's ideas is just as essential. A picture is indeed worth a thousand words, and the presentation of information is enhanced in innumerable ways when accompanied by illustrations, pictures, charts, graphs, and visual media of all kinds.

With this in mind, it is easy to make the case for teaching students how to understand text from representational symbols and how to infuse their own products with representations of the facts that simplify and clarify the communication of their knowledge and understanding of the topic.

Developing representational thinking skills extends into the wonderful world of commanding language, and the ability to produce a rich expression of language opens up possibilities of a variety of career choices—journalism, marketing, communications, science, writing, advertising, singing, art, the list goes on and on.

Examples From the CCSS: Represent

Integration of Knowledge and Ideas: RL.9–10.7. Analyze the representation of a subject or a key scene in two different artistic mediums, including what is emphasized or absent in each treatment (e.g., Auden's "Musée des Beaux Arts" and Breughel's Landscape with the Fall of Icarus.)

Numbers & Operations in Base Ten: 1.NBT.1. Count to 120, starting at any number less than 120. In this range, read and write numerals and represent a number of objects with a written numeral.

TALK THROUGH   Explicit Teaching Lesson

In the Talk-Through, phase I, the educator teaches the thinking skill explicitly. There are several elements to aid the teacher in this phase: motivational mindset, order of operations, instructional strategy, assessment, and metacognitive reflection.

Represent means to stand for, symbolize, or depict. Related terms include *delineate, denote, describe, display, express, hint, illustrate, outline, picture, portray, render,* and *reproduce.*

Motivational Mindset

It is important to break students' propensity to interpret the world around them literally. They must learn to make the distinction between the literal and the figurative. A start is to invite students to take a look at international road signs, and have them discuss with a partner what each sign represents. Visit www.ideamerge.com /motoeuropa/roadsigns for images of European road signs.

Order of Operations

Representing information is a communication skill that students use in every class at one time or another. To help them develop this skill, walk them through the process using the acronym SHOW:

6

Select the idea to represent.

Hunt for significant elements.

Organize elements to show meaning.

Weed for accuracy and impact.

For example, students participate in an exercise about reading body language during which they use the SHOW order of operations. Student pairs are given the task of reading their partner's body language. To do so, they hunt for the elements of body language that portray meaning. They combine these elements to come up with an interpretation of the other student's nonverbal representation. They discuss the consequences of misreading this representation and then role-play such situations.

Instructional Strategy

Optical illusions offer a marvelous example of representing ideas that are both obvious and elusive. Figure 18.1 represents a humorous before-and-after look at the concept of marriage. Using SHOW as the guide, walk the class through the investigation of this illusion.

Figure 18.1: Optical illusion example.

Assessment

Have the students make a checklist of the steps in the SHOW order of operations and then assess how they used each step with the optical illusion.

Metacognitive Reflection

Divide students into trios, and ask them to discuss times when they could use SHOW in their mathematics studies.

WALK THROUGH — Classroom Content Lesson

In the Walk-Through, phase II, teachers practice the thinking skill within content-based lessons, providing guidance to ensure the proper application of the skill. ELA Standard 10 recommends literature and instructional texts that are available for coupling with grade-level lessons.

▶ Elementary Level

Use place value and three-digit numbers in the mathematics lesson to illustrate representation. Use a place value chart to demonstrate that the numeral 145 can be represented as one hundred, four tens, and five ones. Complete the chart to show other combinations (representations). Provide the students with other three-digit numbers, and have them work out the possible combinations in pairs.

▶▶ Middle Level

Design an inquiry lesson that asks students to explore the ways they represent themselves and their values to their peers. The lesson should end with partners sharing a brief presentation of their representation of themselves to each other.

▶▶▶ Secondary Level

Ask students to prepare a presentation that represents their interests, talents, and strengths in reference to college choices and career aspirations. Have them include a section on how they will represent these skills in a college or job interview. Ask them to share their representations with partners.

DRIVE THROUGH — CCSS Performance Task Lesson

During the Drive-Through, phase III, the thinking skill is transferred to authentic applications using CCSS performance tasks, allowing educators to make a direct connection between the selected thinking skill and the new standards. To deepen students' confidence with this skill, the teacher facilitates the student work, moving the students closer and closer to independent practice. Once the students are able to employ the skill independently, they are ready to transfer it across the curriculum. (For additional performance tasks, browse Common Core State Standards, Performance Tasks, Appendix B [NGA & CCSSO, 2010b].)

▶ Elementary Level

The following sample performance task illustrates the application of the ELA standard RL.3.6 (Reading: Literature, grade 3, standard 6):

> When discussing E. B. White's book *Charlotte's Web*, students *distinguish their own point of view* regarding Wilbur the Pig *from* that of Fern Arable as well as *from* that of *the narrator*. (NGA & CCSSO, 2010b, p. 52)

▶▶ Middle Level

The following sample performance task illustrates the application of the ELA standard RI.8.2 (Reading: Informational Text, grade 8, standard 2):

> Students *provide an objective summary of* Frederick Douglass's *Narrative*. They *analyze* how *the central idea* regarding the evils of slavery is *conveyed through supporting ideas* and *developed over the course of the text*. (NGA & CCSSO, 2010b, p. 93)

▶▶▶ Secondary Level

The following sample performance task illustrates the application of the ELA standard RL.9–10.7 (Reading: Literature, grades 9–10, standard 7):

> Students *analyze how* artistic *representations* of Ramses II (the pharaoh who reigned during the time of Moses) vary, basing their analysis on *what is emphasized or absent in different* treatments of the pharaoh in works of art (e.g., images in the British Museum) and in Percy Bysshe Shelley's poem "Ozymandias." (NGA & CCSSO, 2010b, p. 122)

Reflection Questions

These questions are designed to enrich your learning from doing. Such reflection enables you to deepen your understanding of the lessons you have just provided. You might also consider modifying these questions to further guide your students' reflection on this thinking skill.

1. How might you prepare a collaborative assignment in which students represent their thinking in a role play or multimedia project?

2. In mathematics, what progress are you seeing with your students' ability to make mathematical representations?

3. In what other ways can you reinforce the "how to" of representational thinking for your students?

Cognitive Transfer

This proficiency includes skills involved in cognitive transfer and the practical use of what has been transferred. These skills will be used to transfer learning from one setting to another, to apply an idea, concept, or skill in ways that are useful and relevant. A simple example of transfer is learning math facts early in the school curriculum. These facts, once known, are transferred and used in computations and calculations in various school disciplines and in real-world scenarios for the rest of the students' lives.

The three skills included in this proficiency are: (1) synthesize, (2) generalize, and (3) apply. Each contributes to the cognitive transfer of ideas, skills, and concepts. *Synthesizing* requires the blending of component parts to create a whole, leaving one with the core essence of the reading. *Generalizing* describes how the idea travels from one context to the next. For example, formulas taught in math class can later be used to determine how much paint to buy for a room. Finally, *applying* is the skill used to move ideas in the most practical ways.

This proficiency closes the book on the twenty-one selected thinking skills of the CCSS. Each is critical to the ultimate goal of the new standards, which serve to delineate the thinking skills of literacy across the disciplines and into college and career learning.

Chapter 19: Synthesize

James Joyce was a synthesizer, trying to bring in as much as he could. I am an analyzer, trying to leave out as much as I can.

—Samuel Beckett

One day, a youngster captured the synthesis of his grandfather as he sat in his lap. Touching the lines on his grandfather's face, the little one blurted out, "Gramps, your face looks like a road map." In that one sentence, the youngster encapsulated the entire life's journey of the man.

The skill of synthesizing, as positioned in the upper levels of Bloom's taxonomy, often requires a conscious and deliberate mindfulness. Synthesizing is not merely summarizing. It is not retelling, and it is not creating a synopsis of disparate parts. Synthesizing raises the thinking bar to get to the core of the matter. A multinational corporation with positive brand recognition in every corner of the earth is synthesized in three words: "Just Do It!" The monumental effort to communicate the role each citizen plays in the worldwide environmental movement while at the same time empowering everyone everywhere to join the effort is synthesized as "Think Global, Act Local."

Synthesizing is the thinking skill most necessary for creating and building new ideas, products, and performances. Synthesizing encompasses imagination, invention, innovation, and risk taking, which are essential to the creative process. Companies are always searching for a synthesizing term or phrase that will encapsulate the essence of their product or line.

7

Table 19.1 provides examples of what synthesizing looks and sounds like in the classroom.

Table 19.1: Synthesize Look-Fors and Sound Bites

Looks Like	Sounds Like
Students coming up with five words to summarize a story Students creating a symbol to represent a character Students drawing a four-panel cartoon depicting a key concept Students displaying specific artifacts for a field-trip report	"My take on the essence of this is . . ." "A creative blending . . ." "My idea is a synthesis of . . ." "Combining the ideas . . ." "We need a blending, not a mosaic of . . ."

All problem solving and decision making, the macroskills of intelligent behavior, depend on a synthesis of the data, facts, and information. Without the ability to synthesize factors, to blend elements and fuse random thoughts, creativity shuts down.

Examples From the CCSS: Synthesize

Phonics and Word Recognition: RF.5.3,a. Know and apply grade-level phonics and word analysis skills in decoding words.

   a. Use combined knowledge of all letter-sound correspondences, syllabication patterns, and morphology (e.g., roots and affixes) to read accurately unfamiliar multisyllabic words in context and out of context.

Research to Build and Present Knowledge: W.11–12.7. Conduct short as well as more sustained research projects to answer a question (including a self-generated question) or solve a problem; narrow or broaden the inquiry when appropriate; synthesize multiple sources on the subject, demonstrating understanding of the subject under investigation.

TALK   Explicit Teaching Lesson

In the Talk-Through, phase I, the educator teaches the thinking skill explicitly. There are several elements to aid the teacher in this phase: motivational mindset, order of operations, instructional strategy, assessment, and metacognitive reflection.

THROUGH

To *synthesize* is to combine elements into a single entity. Related terms include *blend*, *amalgamate*, *combine*, and *mix*.

Motivational Mindset

Spark interest and curiosity in the higher-order thinking skill of synthesizing using pudding cups. Set a pudding cup on each student's desk, alternating chocolate and vanilla. At the beginning of the class, allow the students to hypothesize about the purpose of the pudding. When they have exhausted their ideas, tell them that the pudding represents a type of thinking that they must learn to do with skill and effectiveness.

Form pairs, with each pair having one cup of vanilla and one of chocolate. Instruct the pairs to synthesize both flavors into one new creation. Offer a supply of containers, utensils, and condiments such as sprinkles, nuts, and raisins. They must be creative in their synthesis and give a name to their final creation. Of course, they can then eat the synthesized creation.

Order of Operations

The acronym BLEND delineates the general steps of the synthesizing process. While the actual process may vary, requiring a longer or shorter version, these steps work well for explicit instruction on how to synthesize ideas in reading, writing, speaking, or listening across all disciplines:

Begin with the big picture.

Look at the elements.

Extract the essence.

Name the nuggets.

Design a seamless image.

For example, student groups are asked to choose a famous slogan and use the BLEND order of operations to create a possible thought process for coming up with the particular slogan. One group chooses Nike's slogan of "Just Do It!" They start with the big picture, Nike sports equipment is what it is all about. Then they look for defining elements and extract the key words that matter. The words that come to mind from past campaigns with Michael Jordon and Tiger Woods, among others, are the words *elite athlete*. Now they name the nuggets, or the ideas projected by Jordon and Woods: actions that get the job done, or just doing the work. This leads to designing a memorable synthesizing slogan around that idea of just doing the work needed to be great, the golden nugget: "Just Do It!"

7

Instructional Strategy

In a specifically designed strategy called "synectics" (Osborn, 1953), synthesis is the key thinking skill used to create what is called a "forced relationship." Synectics is a technique to foster creative combinations that yield unusual or extraordinary results.

Use synectics to introduce students to the skill of synthesizing. Provide each table team with a die and a story grid like figure 19.1. A blank story grid can be found in appendix A on page 194. Have students roll the die for each of the columns to determine their selected elements. For example, if the team rolls a 5 for the Hero column, their hero will be a dentist. Then ask the teams to create a story that blends all of the designated elements. Finally, have the teams write a *TV Guide* synthesis (two to three lines) of the story as if it were to be a television show.

	Hero	Heroine	Villain	Setting	Plot	Resolution
1	Lawyer	Doctor	Sibling	Shop	Kidnapping	Punishment
2	Salesman	Professor	Merchant	Street	Murder	Escape
3	Teacher	Electrician	Broker	Backyard	Argument	Cliff-hanger
4	Webmaster	Editor	Accountant	Lakefront	Death	Happy
5	Dentist	Blogger	Author	High-rise	Surprise	Tragic
6	Musician	Life coach	Banker	House	Fight	Unresolved

Figure 19.1: Story grid example.

Assessment

Ask students to dialogue in an alternating AB partner-talk activity about the BLEND process and whether it is a valuable skill that students need to know. A talks about the B in BLEND, and B talks about the L, and so on, alternating back and forth between the partners.

Metacognitive Reflection

Have students respond to these questions: Are there certain subjects and topics that you find easier to synthesize? If so, what does that tell you about you and your familiarity with those subjects or topics?

WALK THROUGH

Classroom Content Lesson

In the Walk-Through, phase II, teachers practice the thinking skill within content-based lessons, providing guidance to ensure the proper application of the skill. ELA Standard 10 recommends literature and instructional texts that are available for coupling with grade-level lessons.

▶ Elementary Level

Ask students to roll their die five times to generate five random numbers. They find the numbers in the completed math grid, such as that in figure 19.2, and use the operations from the grid to create their equation. They then solve the equation.

For example, a student rolls the following five numbers: 3, 4, 5, 4, 1. After plugging these numbers into the grid, the equation is: $98 + 333 - 9 \times 5 \div 36 = ?$.

A blank math grid can be found in appendix A on page 195.

	+	**−**	**×**	**÷**	**=**
1	694	235	7	4	36
2	2	34	9	3	10
3	98	59	12	2	25
4	1000	333	3	5	78
5	329	326	9	6	99
6	76	48	5	7	100

Figure 19.2: Math grid example.

▶▶ Middle Level

The object of this lesson is to learn different parts of speech and how they are applied in sentences. Ask student groups of three to find examples of adverbs, verbs, adjectives, nouns, prepositions, and conjunctions from material they have been reading. Have them fill in their grid (see figure 19.3, page 168, for an example) with six examples of each part of speech. Once finished, have the teams trade grids with another team, so that they are working with a collection of words they have not seen before. Then they roll the die six times to generate six random numbers, plug in the numbers, learn the words they have to work with, and create a sentence using those words.

7

For example, a team rolls the numbers 4, 3, 2, 6, 5, and 2, resulting in the following words: *hurriedly* (adverb), *sorted* (verb), *pretty* (adjective), *lamp* (noun), *on* (preposition), and *but* (conjunction). They create the following sentence using those words: *Hurriedly,* Sue *sorted* the *pretty* shells *on* the table by the *lamp, but* in her rush to finish, she knocked some on the floor.

A blank parts-of-speech grid can be found in appendix A on page 196.

	Adverb	Verb	Adjective	Noun	Preposition	Conjunction
1	Gingerly	Carried	Colorful	Jar	Over	Yet
2	Spritely	Lifted	Pretty	Suitcase	Under	But
3	Lazily	Sorted	Worn	Chest	Above	However
4	Hurriedly	Walked	Old	Bike	Into	Therefore
5	Lovingly	Shifted	Ugly	Mirror	On	Without
6	Sloppily	Moved	New	Lamp	Beyond	While

Figure 19.3: Parts-of-speech grid example.

▶▶▶ Secondary Level

Have each student roll a single die six times to generate six random numbers and then match these numbers with the appropriate cell in a book-blurb grid (see figure 19.4 for an example). The assignment is to take the elements from the grid and write a one-paragraph description of a book suitable for the book's dust jacket, including a title for the book. Persuasive writing is the objective.

For example, a student who rolled the number 2, 5, 2, 1, 5, and 4 must use a salesman for the hero, a dancer for the heroine, a botched kidnapping for the plot, a battleground for the setting, fantasy for the genre, and pride for the theme. Following is an example of the assignment:

> Book title: *Love Is a Cosmic Battlefield*
>
> Jacket copy: The epic battle between the cyborgs and the humans has raged on for centuries, leaving both worlds exhausted, impoverished, and without hope; but with humans and cyborgs alike too proud to admit defeat, there is no end in sight. Tired of selling cheap laserguns and shoddy used hovertanks just to make a quick buck, smooth-talking salesman Danny Steele devises a scheme to kidnap the cyborg king and bring certain victory to the

humans—and to make him a very, very rich man. But when the kidnapping goes awry, he ends up with Sue Ann as his hostage: the cyborgs' beautiful and haughty ballerina princess. Still, perhaps this mix-up is better than he could have hoped for; that is, if he can keep himself from falling in love with her. And is it his imagination, or behind that pompous façade, does she seem to be falling for him too? Can this unlikely pair bring peace to the cosmic battlefield, or will pride destroy the universe?

A blank book-blurb grid can be found in appendix A on page 197.

	Hero	Heroine	Plot	Setting	Genre	Theme
1	Gentleman	Queen	Failing marriage	Battleground	Romance	Nationalism
2	Salesman	Blogger	Botched kidnapping	Courtroom	Mythology	Fate
3	Boxer	Gentlewomen	Overcoming depression	Hospital	Fable	Isolation
4	Millionaire	Baroness	Pursuit of treasure	Race Track	Tall Tale	Pride
5	General	Dancer	Stormy romance	Ship at Sea	Fantasy	Suffering
6	Statesman	Singer	Planning revenge	Country Home	Mystery	Ambition

Figure 19.4: Book-blurb grid example.

DRIVE CCSS Performance Task Lesson

THROUGH

During the Drive-Through, phase III, the thinking skill is transferred to authentic applications using CCSS performance tasks, allowing educators to make a direct connection between the selected thinking skill and the new standards. To deepen students' confidence with this skill, the teacher facilitates the student work, moving the students closer and closer to independent practice. Once the students are able to employ the skill independently, they are ready to transfer it across the curriculum. In each example, the skill *synthesize* is implied, not explicitly stated. (For additional performance tasks, browse Common Core State Standards, Performance Tasks, Appendix B [NGA & CCSSO, 2010b].)

▶ Elementary Level

The following sample performance task illustrates the application of the ELA standard RL.1.4 (Reading: Literature, grade 1, standard 4):

> Students *identify words and phrases* within Molly Bang's *The Paper Crane* that *appeal to the senses* and *suggest the feelings* of happiness experienced by the owner of the restaurant (e.g., clapped, played, loved, overjoyed). (NGA & CCSSO, 2010b, p. 28)

▶▶ Middle Level

The following sample performance task illustrates the application of the ELA standard RST.6–8.9 (Science & Technical Subjects, grades 6–8, standard 9):

> Students construct a holistic picture of the history of Manhattan by *comparing and contrasting the information gained from* Donald Mackay's *The Building of Manhattan* with the *multimedia sources* available on the "Manhattan on the Web" portal hosted by the New York Public Library (http://legacy.www.nypl.org/branch /manhattan/index2.cfm?Trg=1&d1=865). (NGA & CCSSO, 2010b, p. 100)

▶▶▶ Secondary Level

The following sample performance task illustrates the application of the ELA standard RH.11–12.7 (History/Social Studies, grades 11–12, standard 7):

> Students *integrate* the *information* provided by Mary C. Daly, vice president at the Federal Reserve Bank of San Francisco, with the data presented *visually* in the *FedViews* report. In their analysis of these *sources of information presented in diverse formats,* students frame and *address a question* or *solve a problem* raised by their *evaluation* of the evidence. (NGA & CCSSO, 2010b, p. 183)

Reflection Questions

These questions are designed to enrich your learning from doing. Such reflection enables you to deepen your understanding of the lessons you have just provided. You might also consider modifying these questions to further guide your students' reflection on this thinking skill.

1. How does the grid concept simulate the thinking skill of synthesizing?

2. Determine the relationship between synthesizing information in the world of learning and synthesizing sounds in the world of music. How are they alike and different?

3. How might you use a grid in your classroom to reinforce the process of synthesizing?

4. Complete the following sentence: What has surprised me most about this skill is . . .

7

Chapter 20: Generalize

An idea is always a generalization, and generalization is a property of thinking. To generalize means to think.

> —Georg Wilhelm Friedrich Hegel

A bunch of rowdy kids were playing street hockey on the corner when they were interrupted by an old man yelling at them. He was yelling about everything. "You kids are ruining the neighborhood with all this racket. You are too loud! You are making too much noise! Your game is right in the middle of the street, on all four corners. How is anyone supposed to cross the street? It's not safe! I feel like I am taking my life in my hands when I get near this intersection. Do your mothers know where you are? I doubt they would approve of you playing in the streets like this. Why don't you take your game to the park or to the schoolyard?"

It seemed like they were doing nothing right. Finally, one kid turned to the others and said, "He's just in a bad mood. But he's generally in a bad mood. It's his MO. Don't worry about it. Let's play!"

A generalization is an abstraction of a big idea gleaned from a life situation or from a text. For example, a generalization of the people of Greece is, "The Greeks are great thinkers." Sometimes a qualifying detail is supplied to support the generalization: "After all, they gave us Plato, Aristotle, and Socrates." A generalization is an umbrella-like statement that encompasses the facts, data, and information provided. The idea of the Greeks as great thinkers, because there are great thinkers in Greek history, is an extrapolation of the facts as the speaker knows them.

7

It is important to know that not all generalizations are true. However, heeding the cautionary note to be careful with the use of generalizations, it still is one of the critical skills supporting the cognitive transfer of ideas into practical, relevant, and rich applications.

Table 20.1 provides examples of what generalizing looks and sounds like in the classroom.

Table 20.1: Generalize Look-Fors and Sound Bites

Looks Like	Sounds Like
Students creating an umbrella phrase	"This says it all."
Students determining the big idea of a text	"The big idea . . ."
Students giving historical figures one-word descriptions	"An umbrella theme is . . ."
	"To generalize . . ."
Students making assumptions about an author's collection of works	"My takeaway is . . ."

Generalizing is a higher-order thinking skill that definitely warrants explicit teaching as part of student preparation in the CCSS. It is a skill that allows the learner to take a new idea or emerging understanding and transfer it to other situations. For example, when learning the communication skill of conflict resolution, a student may realize that when negotiating with others during a disagreement, it always helps to start the rebuttal with an affirming statement: "You are absolutely right. This is where we agree. My only concern is how we might find the best alternative for all." In essence, he has learned to generalize a behavior that works.

Another example involves homework. After missing an important deadline on his report and getting a poor grade, a student makes a generalization about procrastinating. He tells his buddy, "I learned my lesson. I know I can't put off doing my homework because I just don't get back to it. I have a new general policy: do it now!" He may apply this generalization to all future instances of possible procrastination.

Generalizations are patterns that are formed based on the big idea that is extrapolated from specific instances. It is a skill of life that helps learners mature in their thinking.

TALK　Explicit Teaching Lesson

In the Talk-Through, phase I, the educator teaches the thinking skill explicitly. There are several elements to aid the teacher in this phase: motivational mindset, order of operations, instructional strategy, assessment, and metacognitive reflection.

THROUGH

To *generalize* is to make an assumption, to draw inferences, to form a conclusion based on generalities. Related terms include *assume, universalize, conclude, judge,* and *determine.*

> ## Examples From the CCSS: Generalize
>
> **Conventions of Standard English: L.2.2,d.** Demonstrate command of the conventions of standard English capitalization, punctuation, and spelling when writing.
>
> > d. Generalize learned spelling patterns when writing words (e.g., *cage → badge*; *boy → boil*).
>
> **Vocabulary Acquisition and Use: L.9–10.4c.** Consult general and specialized reference materials (e.g., dictionaries, glossaries, thesauruses), both print and digital, to find the pronunciation of a word or determine or clarify its precise meaning, its part of speech, or its etymology.

Motivational Mindset

To introduce the skill of generalizing, ask your students to spot overgeneralizations, or "wild-and-woolly claims," that people make. Get them started by asking them to spot the overgeneralizations from the following list by signaling with thumbs up or thumbs down. If it is a wild-and-woolly claim, ask them to tone it down to a more reasonable generalization.

- Everyone is going to the party.
- No other kid has chores.
- All politicians are crooks.
- Nobody else has this early a bedtime.
- Old people forget.
- I never get to do fun things.
- People on TV have better lives than we do.
- Everyone is going on vacation but us.
- This is the worst day of my life.

End with a homework assignment: collect wild-and-woolly claims for a week, and turn in your list for our web page.

Order of Operations

The acronym THEME will help students understand the process of generalizing:

7

Take it all in with the first reading.

Hone in on the key ideas of the piece.

Extrapolate one big (prevailing) idea.

Make a motto or slogan about the big idea.

Express the theme statement.

For example, students read a brief piece about what both Karl Marx and Pope Leo XIII said about child labor. First, they take it all in during the first reading. The piece is about the issue of child labor and how this issue brought Karl Marx and the pope into agreement. Now, they try to hone in on the key points or details that matter: economic pressure turns fathers into slave traders and jeopardizes our future as a society. Next, they skim the piece and try to extrapolate the big idea of all that is presented. The big idea is the impact poverty and market economies have on the family structure. The students then generalize the message and come up with a motto or slogan: Child Labor Hurts. Finally, they create a theme statement to express the big idea in the form of a tagline or refrain: Child Labor Will Cost Society Its Future!

Instructional Strategy

To teach the skill of generalizing, use the activity Themes: Big Idea, Tagline. In this activity, students apply the THEME process to determine the central theme. Following this, they use the skill of generalization to make a statement of the big idea presented in the text or speech.

Choose a topic. Following are some examples based on school level:

- Elementary—plants, space, community, dinosaurs, shapes, words, machines, technology

- Middle—environment, democracy, geometry, social networking, wellness, government, algebra, poetry

- Secondary—19th century English literature, world history, careers, physics, novel study, geography, athletics

Lead table teams through the activity with the following steps:

1. Take in or explore each topic or concept through a brief discussion using TAG (toss around the group) interaction, to include responses from all members. Use a piece of paper crunched into a small ball. *For example, start the discussion off with the topic "cycles." Then have the students toss around the paper ball. Each time a student catches the ball, he or she must add to the discussion of cycles. You may hear such words as* beginning, end, circle, unending path, recurring, repeating, circular, *and* pattern.

2. Hone in on the key details from the conversation and jot them down. *For example, students may jot down, "Circular pattern, no ending, no beginning."*

3. Extrapolate or pull out the big idea or prevailing message from the ongoing discussion. *For example, students may write, "The big idea is that a cycle is a circular repeating pattern."*

4. Make a motto or create a slogan that captures the essence of the topic or concept. *For example, students may come up with, "The end is the beginning! The beginning is the end!"*

5. Express a theme statement that includes the big idea as a tagline. *For example, a team may decide on "Cycles: No End in Sight."*

Assessment

Ask the students to rank the difficulty of this task with a "fist to five" activity. Have them hold up the appropriate number of fingers according to the following and weigh in by explaining why they voted the way they did:

Five fingers—loved the challenge

Four fingers—felt successful

Three fingers—able to do

Two fingers—hard

One finger—struggled

Fist—total frustration

Metacognitive Reflection

Ask students to complete the following analogy: Generalizing is like _____ because both _____.

WALK THROUGH   Classroom Content Lesson

In the Walk-Through, phase II, teachers practice the thinking skill within content-based lessons, providing guidance to ensure the proper application of the skill. ELA Standard 10 recommends literature and instructional texts that are available for coupling with grade-level lessons.

7

▶ Elementary Level

At this level, teach the thinking skill of generalizing as a whole-group activity. Walk the students through the use of THEME with a news article from the local paper. Have them work through the steps guided by your prompts.

▶▶ Middle Level

Ask students to view a film that is scheduled to be on television, explaining that they will be working with the ideas from the film in class. Then guide them through the THEME process of making generalizations. Debrief the class once they have completed the process.

▶▶▶ Secondary Level

Ask students to work with a partner, and assign the task of reading a political blog of their choosing for an entire week. Then have them work through the THEME process for that particular blog, explaining how they would represent this blog to others.

DRIVE CCSS Performance Task Lesson

THROUGH During the Drive-Through, phase III, the thinking skill is transferred to authentic applications using CCSS performance tasks, allowing educators to make a direct connection between the selected thinking skill and the new standards. To deepen students' confidence with this skill, the teacher facilitates the student work, moving the students closer and closer to independent practice. Once the students are able to employ the skill independently, they are ready to transfer it across the curriculum. In each example, the skill of *generalize* is implied, not explicitly stated. (For additional performance tasks, browse Common Core State Standards, Performance Tasks, Appendix B [NGA & CCSSO, 2010b].)

▶ Elementary Level

The following sample performance task illustrates the application of the ELA standard RI.K.2 (Reading: Informational text, kindergarten, standard 2):

> Students (*with prompting and support from the teacher*) read "Garden Helpers" in *National Geographic Young Explorers* and demonstrate their understanding of *the main idea of the text—not all bugs are bad—*by *retelling key details.* (NGA & CCSSO, 2010b, p. 36)

▶▶ Middle Level

The following sample performance task illustrates the application of the ELA standard RL.6.7 (Reading: Literature, grade 6, standard 7):

> Students *compare and contrast* the effect Henry Wadsworth Longfellow's *poem* "Paul Revere's Ride" has on them to the effect they experience from a *multimedia* dramatization of

the event presented in an interactive digital map (http://www
.paulreverehouse.org/ride/), analyzing the impact of different
techniques employed that are *unique to each medium.* (NGA &
CCSSO, 2010b, p. 89)

▶▶▶ Secondary Level

The following sample performance task illustrates the application of the ELA standard RL.11–12.4 (Reading: Literature, grades 11–12, standard 4):

> Students compare and contrast the *figurative and connota-*
> *tive meanings* as well as specific word choices in John Donne's
> "Valediction Forbidding Mourning" and Emily Dickinson's
> "Because I Would Not Stop for Death" in order to *determine*
> *how* the metaphors of the carriage and the compass *shape the*
> *meaning and tone* of each poem. Students *analyze* the ways both
> poets use *language that is particularly fresh, engaging, or beauti-*
> *ful* to convey the *multiple meanings* regarding death contained
> in each *poem.* (NGA & CCSSO, 2010b, p. 163)

Reflection Questions

These questions are designed to enrich your learning from doing. Such reflection enables you to deepen your understanding of the lessons you have just provided. You might also consider modifying these questions to further guide your students' reflection on this thinking skill.

1. How does the skill of generalizing impact student understanding and transfer of learning in your subject area? Across other subject areas?

2. What topics might you use for lessons on generalizing to pique the interest of your students?

3. Complete the following sentence: The most fascinating idea from this chapter is . . .

7

Chapter 21: Apply

I have been impressed with the urgency of doing. Knowing is not enough; we must apply. Being willing is not enough; we must do.

—Leonardo da Vinci

A boy was helping his grandma learn how to send email. She was very excited about her success with Skype and was now motivated to know more about her computer. He showed her how to compose and send an email and even tested it by sending an email back to her computer. He could see she was really interested, and so he also showed her how to send multiple emails at once and even how to send photos. Finally, completely exasperated at the show-and-tell session, she took the mouse from her grandson and said, "Let me have the mouse. I want to do it myself. Until I use it, I won't really know it."

To make use of learning is to apply the learning, the last step of cognitive transfer. This assumes that the understanding is clear and the learning is deep enough to be used in practical, relevant, and meaningful ways. When the ideas, skills, or lessons are applied in purposeful ways, they take on a deeper level of meaning and become solidified. Once one applies a skill or concept, the learning is anchored in a lasting way; it is remembered and retained for future use.

For example, sixth graders learn about the Pythagorean theorem. They can then apply this learning by building a model to see how the theory relates to real-life problems. Eighth graders learn about the Bill of Rights. To apply this learning, they can create simulations and role plays about what happens when those personal rights are infringed upon. That is what applied learning is all about; it is about the experience, the actual realization of the abstract concepts and complex skills.

7

Renate and Geoffrey Caine (Caine, Caine, McClintic, & Klimek, 2008) write about curriculum and the brain and learning. They state that extracurricular activities at the school need to be center stage in the school curriculum. The school newspaper, the yearbook, the daily announcements, the gym demonstration, the science fair, the social studies exhibition, and the school play—these are the applied learning experiences that showcase student learning in authentic ways. These are the examples of purposeful learning that require mastery in the skills of reading, writing, speaking, and listening. Project-based learning should assume an important role in today's classrooms.

Table 21.1 provides examples of what this thinking skill looks and sounds like in the classroom.

Table 21.1: Apply Look-Fors and Sound Bites

Looks Like	Sounds Like
Students carrying out an experiment Students using tools they built Students conversing in a foreign language Students engaged in community project Students constructing a model	"This is not exactly the right way to use this, but . . ." "It's such a practical idea." "I didn't know it would be this easy." "Now, I see how it works." "This really cements it for me."

The skill of applying is, beyond a doubt, one of the most neglected skills in the school curriculum, yet the rationale is overwhelmingly simple: all learning is for transfer!

One of the biggest complaints that teachers hear from students is that they don't see how they will ever use the information or skills they are learning. Their concern has merit to some extent. If all learning is for transfer, then teachers need to provide students with the answer to that very legitimate question: "When am I gonna use this?" When students understand how the lessons they learn in school are applied to real-world situations, the lessons become more valuable to them.

Examples From the CCSS: Apply

Phonics and Word Recognition: RF.K.3. Know and apply grade-level phonics and word analysis skills in decoding words.

Research to Build and Present Knowledge: W.11–12.9a. Apply *grades 11–12 Reading standards* to literature (e.g., "Demonstrate knowledge of eighteenth-, nineteenth- and early-twentieth-century foundational works of American literature, including how two or more texts from the same period treat similar themes or topics").

TALK Explicit Teaching Lesson

In the Talk-Through, phase I, the educator teaches the thinking skill explicitly. There are several elements to aid the teacher in this phase: motivational mindset, order of operations, instructional strategy, assessment, and metacognitive reflection.

THROUGH

To *apply* is to put something to use, to put it into action. Related terms include *utilize, employ, practice, assign, address, use, transfer,* and *implement.*

Motivational Mindset

Have a special guest, who is an expert in sign language, teach the whole class how to say, "I would prefer to not do my homework this week," in sign language. Then tell the class that the first five people who can accurately communicate this message in sign language will be excused from homework.

Order of Operations

The acronym USE delineates the steps of applying skills or concepts to an authentic problem or challenging situation:

Use it in a talk-through.

Simulate it in a guided walk-through.

Extend and employ the learning independently.

For example, students rarely learn to drive by just getting behind the wheel. The students first learn the skills of driving in a classroom setting and using a simulator, with a guide talking them through the various procedures. The students then apply the learning in a somewhat contrived and sterile environment for safety purposes—driving in emptied parking lots and along quiet neighborhood streets with little traffic. When it is deemed that their skill level is such that they can use their skills safely, they do so in a real, on-road situation with moving traffic, road signs, stoplights, exit ramps, and parallel parking spots.

Instructional Strategy

It is important to take the time to come up with possible authentic experiences for students in the classroom. It's one thing to learn about fractions; it's quite another task to apply one's understanding of fractions in designing a scale drawing of the classroom. This kind of hands-on performance task takes a fair amount of time to plan, schedule, organize the materials for, and actually execute with fidelity and assessments. An easy way to approach this is to employ the "talk-through,

7

walk-through, drive-through" strategy, which allows for the gradual release of responsibility to the students.

Start students on the path to writing a five-paragraph essay. Read the following prompts, with appropriate pauses between the steps, as each student responds on paper:

1. Name a good thinker—a fictional character, a historical figure, or a personal acquaintance.

2. Tell two traits of or details about your good thinker.

3. Describe someone who is not a good thinker.

4. Compare and contrast the two.

5. Write a closing statement.

6. Give your piece a telling title.

7. Smooth it out, and when ready, share your reading with a partner.

This talk-through stage does not result in a five-paragraph essay, but it does model the traditional structure of a comprehensive piece of writing.

Now, choose a different topic, and post the prompts on the board or screen. Instruct the students to follow along with the prompts on their own. Tell them that you are providing ten minutes for the exercise. This walk-through stage still does not produce a five-paragraph essay, but the process is becoming clear.

Finally, for the drive-through, the students are assigned a five-paragraph essay on a specific topic but are given no prompts. They are expected to devise their own prompts to guide themselves through the essay.

Assessment

Have the students, in pairs, use the idea of prompts to guide their partner to the completion of a task and apply it to something other than writing. Ask them to provide two examples of where this process would apply.

Metacognitive Reflection

Have the students answer the following question: what have you learned in school that you apply in your everyday life?

WALK THROUGH   Classroom Content Lesson

In the Walk-Through, phase II, teachers practice the thinking skill within content-based lessons, providing guidance to ensure the proper application of the skill. ELA Standard 10 recommends literature and instructional texts that are available for coupling with grade-level lessons.

▶ Elementary Level

Instruct students to draw for one minute on a topic. Then ask them to draw again on the same topic for another minute to revise and refine the first drawing. Repeat the instructions five times so the students can fine-tune the product and apply their skill of rendering with accuracy and precision.

▶▶ Middle Level

Instruct students to write for one minute on a topic. Then ask them to write again on the same topic for another minute to revise and refine the first writing. Repeat the instructions five times so they can fine-tune the product and apply their skill of composing with accuracy and precision.

▶▶▶ Secondary Level

Instruct students to write for one minute on an informational text topic. Then ask them to write again on the same topic for another minute to revise and refine the first writing. Ask the students to exchange their papers with another student, who will then revise and refine the paper. The students then retrieve their original paper to apply a final minute of editing.

DRIVE CCSS Performance Task Lesson

THROUGH

During the Drive-Through, phase III, the thinking skill is transferred to authentic applications using CCSS performance tasks, allowing educators to make a direct connection between the selected thinking skill and the new standards. To deepen students' confidence with this skill, the teacher facilitates the student work, moving the students closer and closer to independent practice. Once the students are able to employ the skill independently, they are ready to transfer it across the curriculum. In each example, the skill of *apply* is implied, not explicitly stated. (For additional performance tasks, browse Common Core State Standards, Performance Tasks, Appendix B [NGA & CCSSO, 2010b].)

▶ Elementary Level

The following sample performance task illustrates the application of the ELA standard RI.3.3 (Reading: Informational Text, grade 3, standard 3):

> Students read Robert Coles's retelling of *a series of historical events* in *The Story of Ruby Bridges. Using* their knowledge of how *cause and effect* gives order to *events*, they *use* specific *language* to *describe* the *sequence* of events that leads to Ruby desegregating her school. (NGA & CCSSO, 2010b, p. 62)

7

▶▶ Middle Level

The following sample performance task illustrates the application of the ELA standard RST.6–8.3 (Science & Technical Subjects, grades 6–8, standard 3):

> Students learn about fractal geometry by reading Ivars Peterson and Nancy Henderson's *Math Trek: Adventures in the Math Zone* and then generate their own fractal geometric structure by *following the multistep procedure* for creating a Koch's curve. (NGA & CCSSO, 2010b, p. 100)

▶▶▶ Secondary Level

The following sample performance task illustrates the application of the ELA standard RST.11–12.4 (Science & Technical Subjects, grades 11–12, standard 4):

> Students *determine the meaning of key terms* such as *hydraulic, trajectory,* and *torque* as well as other *domain-specific words and phrases* such as *actuators, antilock brakes,* and *traction control used* in Mark Fischetti's "Working Knowledge: Electronic Stability Control." (NGA & CCSSO, 2010b, p. 183)

Reflection Questions

These questions are designed to enrich your learning from doing. Such reflection enables you to deepen your understanding of the lessons you have just provided. You might also consider modifying these questions to further guide your students' reflection on this thinking skill.

1. List specific examples of performance tasks that you use successfully to illustrate the application and transfer of skills to real-world situations.

2. How might you address the application of learning in a more explicit way?

3. What skills do you teach your students that they will apply in their daily lives five years after they leave your classroom?

Appendix A: Reproducibles

Fishbone Diagram

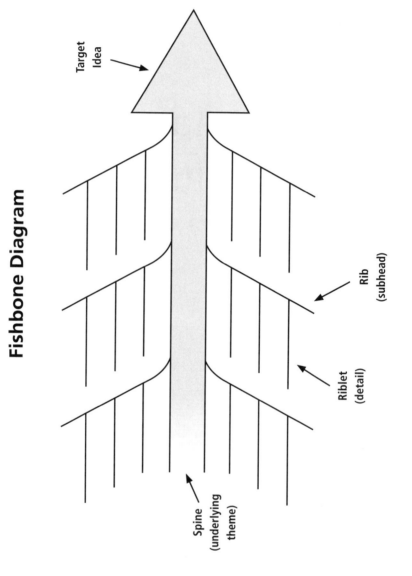

Target
Idea

Rib
(subhead)

Riblet
(detail)

Spine
(underlying
theme)

Ranking Ladder

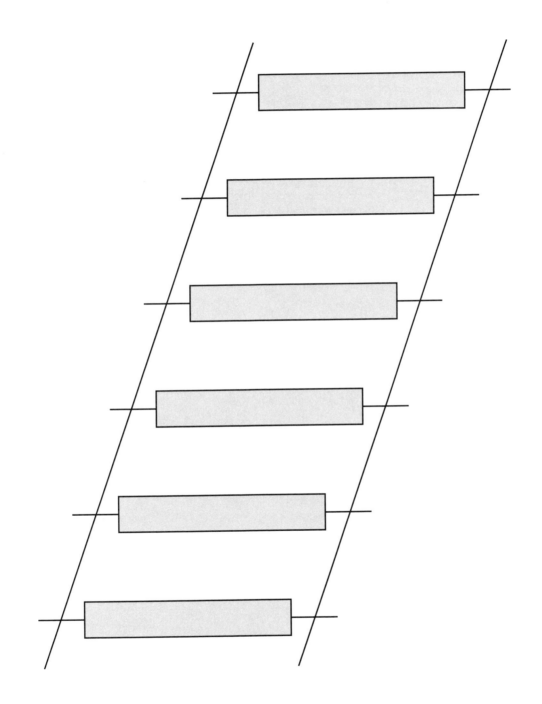

Four-Fold Concept Development

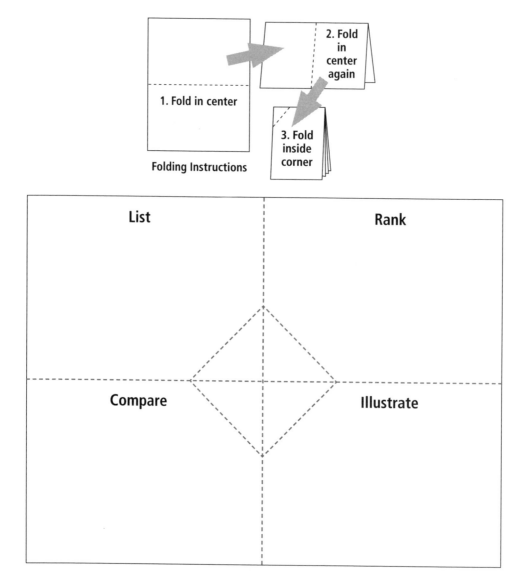

Folding Instructions

1. Fold in center

2. Fold in center again

3. Fold inside corner

List

Rank

Compare

Illustrate

ABC Graffiti

Topic:

A	N
B	O
C	P
D	Q
E	R
F	S
G	T
H	U
I	V
J	W
K	X
L	Y
M	Z

Comic Strip Template

Draw the opening scene.	Draw the characters described.	Draw the plot or setup.	Draw the actual event.	Draw people reacting.	Draw the punch line.

KWL Chart

K What I Know	W What I Want to Know	L What I Learned

Story Grid

	Hero	Heroine	Villain	Setting	Plot	Resolution
1						
2						
3						
4						
5						
6						

Math Grid

	+	–	×	÷	=
1					
2					
3					
4					
5					
6					

Parts-of-Speech Grid

	Adverb	Verb	Adjective	Noun	Preposition	Conjunction
1						
2						
3						
4						
5						
6						

Book-Blurb Grid

	Hero	Heroine	Plot	Setting	Genre	Theme
1						
2						
3						
4						
5						
6						

Appendix B:
Additional Resources

Books and Articles

Barrows, H. (1985). *How to design a problem-based curriculum for preclinical years.* New York: Springer.

Bellanca, J. (2010). *Enriched learning projects: A practical pathway to 21st century skills.* Bloomington, IN: Solution Tree Press.

Bellanca, J., & Brandt, R. (Eds.). (2010). *21st century skills: Rethinking how students learn.* Bloomington, IN: Solution Tree Press.

Bellanca, J., & Stirling, T. (2011). *Classrooms without borders: Using Internet projects to teach communication and collaboration.* New York: Teachers College Press.

Bloom, B., Englehart, M. D., Furst, E. J., Hill, W. H., & Krathwohl, D. (1956). *Taxonomy of educational objectives handbook I: The cognitive domain.* New York: Longman.

Brookhart, S. M. (2010). *How to assess higher-order thinking skills in your classroom.* Alexandria, VA: Association for Supervision and Curriculum Development.

Burke, K. (2006). *From standards to rubrics in 6 steps: Tools for assessing student learning, K–8.* Thousand Oaks, CA: Corwin Press.

Burke, K. (2010). *Balanced assessment: From formative to summative.* Bloomington, IN: Solution Tree Press.

Costa, A. L., & Liebman, R. M. (Eds.). (1997). *Supporting the spirit of learning: When process is content.* Thousand Oaks, CA: Corwin Press.

Coyle, D. (2009). *The talent code: Greatness isn't born. It's grown. Here's how.* New York: Bantam Books.

Darling-Hammond, L. (2010). *The flat world and education: How America's commitment to equity will determine our future.* New York: Teachers College Press.

de Bono, E. (1973). *CoRT thinking*. Blandford, England: Direct Educational Services.

de Bono, E. (1993). *Teach your child how to think*. London: Penguin.

Dede, C. (2010). Comparing frameworks for 21st century skills. In J. A. Bellanca & R. Brandt (Eds.), *21st century skills: Rethinking how students learn* (pp. 51–76). Bloomington, IN: Solution Tree Press.

Drucker, P. (1959). Long-range planning: Challenge to management science. *Management Science, 5*(3), 238–249.

DuFour, R., & DuFour, R. (2010). The role of 21st century skills in advancing professional learning communities. In J. A. Bellanca & R. Brandt (Eds.), *21st century skills: Rethinking how students learn* (pp. 77–96). Bloomington, IN: Solution Tree Press.

Dweck, C. (2007). *Mindset: The new psychology of success*. New York: Random House.

Fogarty, R. (1997). *Problem-based learning and other curriculum models for the multiple intelligences classroom*. Arlington Heights, IL: IRI/Skylight Training.

Fogarty, R., & Bellanca, J. (1987). *Patterns for thinking, patterns for transfer: A cooperative team approach for critical and creative thinking in the classroom*. Palatine, IL: IRI/Skylight.

Fogarty, R., & Pete, B. (2007). *From staff room to classroom: A guide for planning and coaching professional development*. Thousand Oaks, CA: Corwin Press.

Fogarty, R., & Pete, B. (2010). *Supporting differentiated instruction: A professional learning communities approach*. Bloomington, IN: Solution Tree Press.

Frost, R. (2011). *The span of life*. Accessed at www.americanpoems.com/poets/robertfrost/5540 on January 19, 2011.

Fullan, M., & Hargreaves, A. (Eds.). (2008). *Change wars*. Bloomington, IN: Solution Tree Press.

Gardner, H. (2007). *Five minds for the future*. Boston: Harvard Business School Press.

Goleman, D. (1996). *Emotional intelligence: Why it can matter more than IQ*. New York: Bantam Dell.

Hattie, J. (2008). *Visible learning: A synthesis of over 800 meta-analyses relating to achievement*. New York: Routledge.

Kao, J. (2007). *Innovation nation: How America is losing its innovation edge, why it matters, and what we can do to get it back*. New York: Free Press.

Kolderie, T., & McDonald, T. (2009). *How information technology can enable 21st century schools*. Washington, DC: Information Technology and Innovation Foundation.

Joyce, B., & Showers, B. (1987). *Power in staff development through research on training*. Alexandria, VA: Association for Supervision and Curriculum Development.

Joyce, B., & Showers, B. (2002). *Student achievement through staff development*. Alexandria, VA: Association for Supervision and Curriculum Development.

McGregor, D. (2007). *Developing thinking, developing learning: A guide to thinking skills in education*. Berkshire, England: Open University Press.

McTighe, J., & Seif, E. (2010). An implementation framework to support 21st century skills. In J. A. Bellanca & R. Brandt (Eds.), *21st century skills: Rethinking how students learn* (pp. 149–174). Bloomington, IN: Solution Tree Press.

National Governors Association Center for Best Practices & Council of Chief State Officers. (2010). *Common core state standards for English language arts & literacy in history/ social studies, science, and technical subjects*. Accessed at www .corestandards.org/assets/CCSSI_ELA%20Standards.pdf on December 16, 2011.

Parnes, S. J. (1975). *Aha! Insights into creative behavior*. New York: D.O.K.

Partnership for 21st Century Skills. (2009). *Framework for 21st century learning*. Tucson, AZ: Author.

Perkins, D. N., & Salomon, G. (1988). Teaching for transfer. *Educational Leadership, 46*(1), 22–32.

Pink, D. (2009). *Drive: The surprising truth about what motivates us*. New York: Riverhead Books.

Ravitch, D. (2010). *Stop the madness*. Washington, DC: National Education Association.

Resnick, L. B. (1987). *Education and learning to think*. Washington, DC: National Academies Press.

Schlechty, P. C. (2009). *Leading for learning: How to transform schools into learning organizations*. San Francisco: Jossey-Bass.

Simon, S. (2006). *Volcanoes*. New York: HarperCollins.

Strunk, W., Jr., & White, E. B. (1979). *The elements of style* (3rd ed.). New York: Macmillan.

Toffler, A. (1970). *Future shock*. New York: Bantam Books.

Tucker, M. C. (2008). Industrial benchmarking: A research method for education. In M. Fullan & A. Hargreaves (Eds.), *Change wars* (pp. 117–134). Bloomington, IN: Solution Tree Press.

Twilling, B., & Fadel, C. (2009). *21st century skills: Learning for life in our times*. San Francisco: Jossey-Bass.

Wagner, T. (2008). *The global achievement gap: Why even our best schools don't teach the new survival skills our children need—and what we can do about it*. New York: Basic Books.

Wiggins, G., & McTighe, J. (2005). *Understanding by design* (expanded 2nd ed.). Alexandria, VA: Association for Supervision and Curriculum Development.

Willis, J. (2006). *Research-based strategies to ignite student learning: Insights from a neurologist and classroom teacher*. Alexandria, VA: Association for Supervision and Curriculum Development.

Willis, J. (2008a). *How your child learns best: Brain-friendly strategies you can use to ignite your child's learning and increase school success*. Naperville, IL: Sourcebooks.

Willis, J. (2008b). *Teaching the brain to read: Strategies for improving fluency, vocabulary, and comprehension*. Alexandria, VA: Association for Supervision and Curriculum Development.

Willis, J. (2010a). *Learning to love math: Teaching strategies that change student attitudes and get results*. Alexandria, VA: Association for Supervision and Curriculum Development.

Willis, J. (2010b). The current impact of neuroscience on teaching and learning. In D. A. Sousa (Ed.), *Mind, brain, & education: Neuroscience implications for the classroom* (pp. 45–68). Bloomington, IN: Solution Tree Press.

Technology Tools

Technology used to manage, operate, govern, and instruct is a key indicator of a 21st century school. This list identifies specific sites used by school administrators, teachers, and students who are prolific users of technology in their schoolwork life (visit **go.solution-tree.com/commoncore** to access links to the websites in this book):

- Audacity (www.audacity.sourceforge.net)—Offers a sound editor and recording software

- Classroom 2.0 (www.classroom20.com)—A social media site, a collaborative network for educators; offers multiple tools

- Classtools.net (www.classtools.net)—Allows educators to create a variety of tools for classroom use

- CmapTools (http://cmap.ihmc.us)—Offers tools for creating concept maps

- Creaza (www.creaza.com)—Offers a suite of online tools that students can use to create, publish, and share digital stories, in and out of school; premium version has a fee
- ePals (www.epals.com)—An international K–12 social network site with school mail, projects, and collaborations
- ePortfolio (www.eportfolio.org)—Allows for the creation of an online portfolio
- FreeMind (http://freemind.sourceforge.net)—Open-source tool; offers mind-mapping software
- Google Docs (http://docs.google.com)—A collaborative site where students and teachers can create and share work online and access documents from anywhere; documents include spreadsheets, presentations, surveys, and more
- Intel® Teach Program(www.intel.com/about/corporateresponsibility/education/programs/intelteach_us/index.htm)—Online courses for teachers to develop 21st century skills
- JumpStart (www.jumpstart.com)—Offers 3-D virtual-world games
- Kerpoof (http://kerpoof.com)—Multimedia software used to create original artwork, animated movies, stories, greeting cards, and so on
- Mind42 (www.mind42.com)—An online mind-map collaboration tool
- Moodle (http://moodle.org)—A content management tool and community site for online learning
- Ning (www.ning.com)—An online service to create, customize, and share a social network
- Partnership for 21st Century Skills (www.p21.org)—Offers multiple resources to help schools transfer to a 21st century agenda
- Podbean (www.podbean.com)—A podcast publishing and social subscribing site; students can publish their own podcasts
- Poll Everywhere (www.polleverywhere.com)—A student response system
- ReadWriteThink.org (www.readwritethink.org)—Offers online tools, tactics, and strategies to develop students' CCSS-aligned language arts skills
- Second Life (http://secondlife.com)—A virtual world that offers avatars, chat, and online meetings
- Shelfari (www.shelfari.com)—A social network for people who love books
- SimCEO (www.simceo.org)—A simulation site; students create and operate their own companies while advancing financial literacy
- SurveyMonkey (www.surveymonkey.com)—Software for conducting online questionnaires and surveys; results can be shown numerically or graphically

- Wikispaces (www.wikispaces.com)—Offers wikis for individuals or groups
- Wordle (www.wordle.net)—Offers the generation of "word clouds" from text

Websites

Educators may find the following websites useful as informational sources or for planning and executing lessons:

- Buck Institute for Education (www.bie.org)
- Common Core State Standards (www.corestandards.org)
- Cooperative Learning Institute (www.co-operation.org)
- Educational Testing Service (www.ets.org)
- EducationWorld; National Standards (www.educationworld.com/standards)
- Edutopia (www.edutopia.org)
- International Renewal Institute, Inc. (www.iriinc.us)
- International Society for Technology in Education: Standards (www.iste.org/standards.aspx)
- Khan Academy (www.khanacademy.org)
- Learning Forward (formerly National Staff Development Council) (www.learningforward.org)
- Massachusetts Curriculum Frameworks (www.doe.mass.edu/frameworks/current.html)
- National Education Technology Plan, 2010 (www2.ed.gov/technology/plan)
- New Tech Network (www.newtechnetwork.org)
- Thinkfinity (www.thinkfinity.org)

Glossary

anchor standards. A framework for the ELA standards in the CCSS that guides the generic elements for the standards at the various grade levels (for example, key ideas and details, craft and structure, integration of knowledge and ideas, and range of reading and level of complexity).

application. The act of putting a basic skill or mental operation into practice.

balanced assessment. An approach that includes the assessment of both the cognitive skill that processes the content of a standard and knowledge of the actual subject-matter content.

cognitive function. A mental ability that prepares the learner to put thinking and problem solving into action.

cognitive transfer. The mental act of moving learned concepts or skills from the mind to real-world practice; the student proficiency that includes the skills of synthesize, generalize, and apply.

collaborative thinking. The student proficiency that includes the skills of explain, develop, and decide.

Common Core State Standards (CCSS). The Common Core State Standards for English Language Arts and Literacy in History/Social Studies and Science & Technical Subjects, and for Mathematics are broad-based K–12 standards intended to guide schools in making students college and career ready.

communicative thinking. The student proficiency that includes the skills of reason, connect, and represent.

complex thinking. The student proficiency that includes the skills of clarify, interpret, and determine.

comprehensive thinking. The student proficiency that includes the skills of understand, infer, and compare and contrast.

concept development. The intentional development of abstract ideas from specific instances or concrete actions.

connotation. A variety of meanings suggested or implied by a word.

content. The concepts, skills, facts, and/or ideas that comprise a subject matter within an academic discipline.

cooperative learning. A highly effective instructional strategy defined by five key attributes (positive interdependence, individual accountability, group reflection, explicit social skills, face-to-face discussion with a shared goal) and most commonly used to strengthen collaboration skills in the classroom.

creative thinking. The student proficiency that includes the skills of generate, associate, and hypothesize.

critical thinking. The student proficiency that includes the skills of analyze, evaluate, and problem solve.

deep understanding. This is the result of students making sense of ideas and finding the underlying meaning in data or texts they are examining.

denotation. The literal definition of a word.

direct instruction. A model of instruction that uses teacher-directed lessons with specific procedures detailed in a recommended sequential order.

Drive-Through. Third phase of the explicit teaching model; it requires students to work independently on a performance task in CCSS to show evidence of learning.

explicit teaching. An approach to teaching that identifies and targets a specific behavior or skill in the standards and uses formal, teacher-directed instruction and assessment.

formative assessment. A range of formal and informal assessment procedures employed by teachers during the learning process in order to modify teaching and learning strategies with a goal to increase student achievement or the development of 21st century skills.

high-frequency words. The thinking skills that appear most frequently within the Common Core State Standards.

ill-defined problem. Also called a loosely structured or messy problem, the elements of this problem lack clarity, and the relationship of parts to the whole is difficult to define. Ill-defined problems may be extremely complex and encompass many cultural conflicts or involve many teaching and learning disciplines.

innovation. The result of a thinking process that uses both critical and creative thinking skills to produce an invention or a new process or method for making a new product.

inquiry. A process that requires investigation, experimentation, or exploration to answer a question or solve a problem. In project-based learning scenarios, the investigation will proceed through three phases: gathering information, making sense of that information, and communicating the findings.

instructional strategy. The method a teacher may take to achieve a learning objective.

look-for. Observable, specific behavior that a teacher can see or hear as students work in the classroom.

mental operation. An operation, or way of thinking, that helps form ideas.

metacognitive reflection. A mental process of intentionally thinking about one's thinking as a way of assessing the development of a thinking function or cognitive operation; awareness and control over one's thinking.

performance task. A task given to students in phase III, the Drive-Through, with decreasing scaffolding so that students can show increasing competence in their ability to apply a stated thinking skill to a standard's stated content.

PISA. Programme for International Student Assessment is an international test taken by members in the Organisation for Economic Cooperation and Development. The United States is one of thirty members. The computer-based test is presented every three years to countries choosing to participate in all or one framework offered (literacy, mathematical problem solving, cross-curricular problem solving, science literacy, and financial literacy).

problem-based learning. This is an inquiry model of standards-aligned instruction that starts with a loosely structured, authentic problem and ends with a solution to that problem. Students complete activities that allow them to find and apply the information needed to proceed throughout the problem-solving endeavor.

problem scenario. A statement of an open-ended problem that includes a stakeholder role.

problem solving. A comprehensive cognitive act that combines the use of several thinking skills to move from the definition of the problem to its solution.

project-based learning. A model of standards-aligned instruction that starts with an essential question of authentic interest to the students. Students systematically gather information, make sense of the information, and then decide how to communicate their new understandings. Project-based learning typically concludes with a product that shows the rigor of their study via a presentation to an invited audience.

sound bite. A term used to describe a quick description of what a thinking behavior sounds like.

stakeholder role. Stakeholders are those who have an interest in an outcome, who affect or can be affected by an action. Parents, teachers, and other caregivers are significant stakeholders in the students' education.

Talk-Through. First phase of the explicit teaching model; it requires a direct instruction lesson or an inquiry lesson with step-by-step scaffolding to teach a cognitive process for a thinking skill.

technology tool. Hardware, software, and Internet sites and applications that teachers can include in lessons and projects to enrich student learning.

transfer of learning. Occurs when learning in one context enhances (positive transfer) or undermines (negative transfer) a related performance in another context.

Walk-Through. Second phase of the explicit teaching model; it requires a teacher-guided classroom lesson that provides the needed support and scaffolding—guided practice that precedes independent practice.

well-defined problem. Also called a clean or tight problem, the elements of the problem statement are specific and clearly defined within one teaching and learning discipline or real-world situation. The most well-defined problems are found in mathematics.

References and Resources

Allard, H., & Marshall, J. (1997). *Miss Nelson is missing.* Boston: Houghton Mifflin.

American Management Association. (2010). *AMA 2010 critical skills survey.* Accessed at www.p21.org/storage/documents/Critical%20Skills%20Survey%20 Executive%20Summary.pdf on April 2, 2012.

Anderson, R. C., Hiebert, E., Scott, J., & Wilkinson, I. (1984). *Becoming a nation of readers: The report of the commission on reading.* Pittsburgh, PA: National Academy of Education.

Atkins, J., & Fisher, M. (2010). *South Australian teaching for effective learning framework guide.* Adelaide, South Australia: Government of South Australia.

Atkins, J., & Fisher, M. (2011). *South Australian teaching for effective learning review tools handbook.* Adelaide, South Australia: Government of South Australia.

Ausubel, D. P. (1960). The use of advance organizers in the learning and retention of meaningful verbal material. *Journal of Educational Psychology, 51*(5), 267–272.

Bach, R. (2002). *Writer ferrets: Chasing the muse (Ferret chronicles #3).* New York: Scribner.

Bacon, F. (1625). *Of studies.* Accessed at www.authorama.com/essays-of-francis -bacon-50.html on April 2, 2012.

Bellanca, J., & Fogarty, R. (2003). *Blueprints for thinking in the cooperative classroom* (3rd ed.). Glenview, IL: Pearson Education.

Browne, J. (1972) *Jackson Browne* [Album]. New York: Asylum Records.

Caine, R., Caine, G., McClintic, C., & Klimek, K. (2008). *12 Mind/brain principles in action.* Thousand Oaks, CA: Corwin Press.

Costa, A. L., & Kallick, B. (Eds.). (2000). *Discovering and exploring habits of mind.* Alexandria, VA: Association for Supervision and Curriculum Development.

Deming, W. E. (1982). *Out of the crisis*. Cambridge, MA: Massachusetts Institute of Technology.

Feuerstein, R., Feuerstein, R. S., & Falik, L. H. (2010). *Beyond smarter: Mediated learning and the brain's capacity for change*. New York: Teachers College Press.

Feuerstein, R., Rand, Y., Hoffman, M. B., & Miller, R. (1980). *Instrumental enrichment: An intervention program for cognitive modifiability*. Baltimore: University Park Press.

Fischer, M.H. (n.d.). *BrainyQuotes: Martin H. Fischer quotes*. Accessed at www .brainyquote.com/quotes/quotes/m/martinhfi402160.html on May 8, 2012.

Fisher, D., & Frey, N. (2008). *Better learning through structured teaching: A framework for the gradual release of responsibility*. Alexandria, VA: Association for Supervision and Curriculum Development.

Hall, G. E. (1979). The concerns-based approach to facilitating change. *Educational Horizons, 57*(4), 202–208.

Hunter, M. (1971). *Teach for transfer*. Thousand Oaks, CA: Corwin Press.

Jervis, K., & Tobier, A. (Eds.). (1988). *Education for democracy: Proceedings from the Cambridge School Conference on Progressive Education, October, 1987*. Weston, MA: Cambridge School.

Johnson, D., & Johnson, R. (1975). *Learning together and alone: Cooperation, competition, and individualization*. Englewood Cliffs, NJ: Prentice Hall.

Johnson, D., & Johnson, R. (1981). Effects of cooperative and individualistic learning experiences on interethnic interaction. *Journal of Educational Psychology, 73*(3), 444–449.

Johnson, D., & Johnson, R. (2010). Cooperative learning and conflict resolution: Essential 21st century skills. In J. A. Bellanca & R. Brandt (Eds.), *21st century skills: Rethinking how students learn* (pp. 201–220). Bloomington, IN: Solution Tree Press.

Joyce, B., & Weil, M. (1995). *Models of teaching* (5th ed.). New York: Allyn & Bacon.

Kagan, S. (1994). *Cooperative learning*. San Clemente, CA: Kagan.

Kao, J. (2007). *Innovation nation: How America is losing its innovation edge, why it matters, and what we can do to get it back*. New York: Free Press.

Marzano, R. J. (1991). Fostering thinking across the curriculum through knowledge restructuring. *Journal of Reading, 34*(7), 518–525.

Mike Tyson (n.d.). *BrainyQuote: Mike Tyson quotes*. Accessed at www.brainyquote .com/quotes/authors/m/mike_tyson_3.html on May 8, 2012.

Marzano, R. J., Pickering, D. J., & Pollock, J. E. (2001). *Classroom instruction that works: Research-based strategies for increasing student achievement.* Alexandria, VA: Association for Supervision and Curriculum Development.

National Governors Association Center for Best Practices & Council of Chief State School Officers. (2010a). *Common core state standards.* Washington, DC: Author. Accessed at www.corestandards.org on April 2, 2012.

National Governors Association Center for Best Practices & Council of Chief State School Officers. (2010b). *Common core state standards for English language arts & literacy in history/social studies science, and technical subjects: Appendix B: Text exemplars and sample performance tasks.* Washington, DC: Author. Accessed at www.corestandards.org/assets/Appendix_B.pdf on April 2, 2012.

National Governors Association Center for Best Practices and Council of Chief State School Officers. (2010c). *Common core state standards for mathematics.* Washington, DC: Authors. Accessed at www.corestandards.org/assets/CCSSI_Math%20Standards.pdf on April 2, 2012.

Ogle, D.M. (1986). K-W-L: A teaching model that develops action reading of expository text. *Reading Teacher, 39*(6), 564–570.

Osborn, A. (1953). *Applied imagination: Principles and procedures of creative problem solving.* New York: Scribner.

Partnership for 21st Century Skills. (2011). *Framework for 21st century learning.* Accessed at www.p21.org on March 26, 2012.

Pete, B., & Fogarty, R. (2009). *From staff room to classroom II: The one-minute professional development planner.* Thousand Oaks, CA: Corwin Press.

Programme for International Student Assessment. (2009). *PISA 2009 technical report.* Accessed at www.oecd.org/document/19/0,3746,en_2649 _35845621_48577747_1_1_1_1,00.html on April 2, 2012.

Programme for International Student Assessment. (2012) *Framework for PISA 2012 problem solving.* Paris, France: Organisation for Economic Co-operation and Development.

Schmoker, M. (1999). *Results: The key to continuous school improvement* (2nd ed.). Alexandria, VA: Association for Supervision and Curriculum Development.

Science Buddies. (n.d.). *Steps of the scientific method.* Accessed at www.sciencebuddies .org/science-fair-projects/project_scientific_method.shtml on January 11, 2012.

Sharan, S. (Ed.). (1990). *Cooperative learning: Theory and research.* New York: Praeger.

Slavin, R. (1996). *Education for all.* New York: Swets & Zeitlinger.

Torrance, E. P. (1974). *Torrance test of creative thinking.* New York: Scholastic Testing Service.

Tuchman, B. (1965). *Developmental sequence in small groups. Psychological Bulletin, 63*(6), 384–399. Washington, DC: American Psychological Association.

Wayman, J. (1980). *The other side of reading.* New York: Good Apple.

Webb, A. (2011, January 11). The thoughtful parent: The power of words [Web log post]. Accessed at www.thoughtfulparent.com/2011/01/power-of-words .html on December 16, 2011.

Index

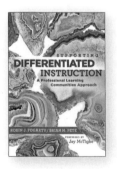